TAILGATING HANDBOOK

The Gear, The Food, The Stadiums

STEPHEN LINN

[interactive blvd]™

An Interactive Blvd Book

theultimatetailgater.com

CONTENTS

Photo: Scott Eklund

TAILGATE USA

Americans love their parking lots. Okay, not so much the parking lot itself, but what we do there before football games.

Tailgating is a part of our social fabric. For many of us, our tailgate neighborhoods are as important to us as the neighborhoods we live in. And we often like our tailgate neighbors better. We don't picnic in America any more; we tailgate.

Don't believe me? Just look in the parking lots and fields around places like Green Bay and Kansas City, Knoxville and Happy Valley. Still don't believe me? Then look at the numbers.

This year more than 50 million Americans will tailgate at a football game. That's about one of every five of us. That's more people than *live* in Spain.

And we're not talking just about tailgating at a game or two. An American Tailgaters Association survey found that almost half of tailgaters tailgate at least six times a season and throw their parking lot parties with 10–39 of their friends.

Photo: Bruce Newman

Of course, part of the fun of tailgating is that you're also partying with thousands of people you don't know. But you feel like you do. In addition to the fun of tailgating itself, it is also an activity that brings communities together behind a common goal—beat your opponent. In NFL parking lots you find high-dollar CEOs sharing ribs with construction workers. College tailgates find students and alumni filling each other's glasses. You're not going to find them doing that anywhere else.

There is a communal passion among tailgaters. It's hard to explain to people who haven't experienced it, but once you've tailgated you tend to want to go back again. And again.

But how did our nation become Tailgate USA?

Some historians tell me the first tailgate party was on July 21, 1861, at Bull Run. Yep, that Bull Run—the first major land battle of the Civil War. Spectators came to see Union and Confederate troops fight. Great idea, horrible application; war really isn't the best spectator sport.

A better one came along about eight years later in New Brunswick, New Jersey, when Rutgers University and the College of New Jersey

Photo: JC Ridley

(now Princeton University) battled on the football field. It's this game on November 6, 1869, that's considered the first intercollegiate football game and the first tailgate party in the sense that we think of them today. Fans laid out picnic lunches and watched The Scarlet take home a win "6 runs to 4." (Rutgers wasn't called the Scarlet Knights until 1955.)

Tailgating became more popular around the turn of the century as cars became more popular. After all, it's easier to take your friends and your food to a game in a car than on a horse. But it wouldn't be until the 1970s that tailgating truly took hold and started on its path to becoming an American pastime. That, of course, was the era of the big station wagons and their big tailgates.

The first station wagons looked like, well, wagons. During the early part of the 20th century these "depot hacks," as they were often called, carried people and luggage from train stations to various places in town. From that came the name "station wagon."

But it was station wagons with names like the Ford Country Squire and Chevrolet Caprice that became popular in the 1960s and 1970s, caught our imaginations, and filled parking lots outside stadiums across the country. You could fit a lot of food in those wagons, and the tailgates made for perfect buffet tables.

During this same time backyard grilling became an American obsession. In great part you can thank George Stephen for that. You may not know the metalworker's name, but when he inherited the Weber Bros. Metal Spinning Co. that made harbor buoys he decided to make some modifications. He cut a buoy in half, added a grate, cut vents into the top, and used it as a lid. And that's how the Weber grill was born.

It was only a matter of time before the car, the grill, and the party converged in a parking lot. And when they did, they'd park next to an RV.

RVs are another tool of ultimate tailgaters. As these movable houses became more popular and better outfitted in the 1980s and 1990s, they offered another way to kick up the tailgate party a notch.

When you add all of this together with food, gear, licensed products, and the like, tailgating has become a multibillion dollar industry. There's even a tailgating trade show now.

The good news for you is that the book in your hands is going to help you pick the right gear, cook some great food, and have a great time at your tailgate party. It will also help you know where to set up your party. The "Where to Tailgate" chapter has venue guides for every NFL and NCAA Division I-A team in the country, including tips and rules for tailgating and some facts to help you win a bet with those tailgating next to you.

Photo: Ed Rode

THE STUFF YOU NEED

The basics are simple. Your tailgate party needs something to eat, something to drink, something to sit on, and atmosphere. But it isn't *really* that simple.

Now that tailgating has become a national pastime, as well as big business, you have a lot of options to sort through and tools to evaluate. While you do need the right tools to tailgate, you don't need to have the biggest rig in the parking lot to throw a great party. Sure, that $3,000 portable kitchen and flatbed living room with plasma TVs are impressive, but you can cook some mean ribs on a charcoal kettle grill and enjoy them sitting in a fold-away canvas chair, too.

Of course the centerpiece of your tailgate party is the food, and a main ingredient is a grill. You'll need one, but what type? For most of us our first decision is a classic one: gas or charcoal. (There are plenty of other options now; check out "What's a Grill to Do?" to learn about them.)

This battle is really about taste versus convenience. Charcoalers will tell you food is more flavorful off of their grills. They're right. Gas grillers will tell you there's nothing easier at a tailgate party than pushing a button and having your grill ready in just a few minutes. They're right.

I can't make that decision for you, but I can help you get the best grill for your needs.

Before you head to the store, ask yourself a few questions:

1. How often will I tailgate?

2. Will I use the grill for only tailgating or for backyard cookouts, too?

3. What's my budget?

4. How important are all those optional features?

5. How many people will I feed and how much cooking space do I need to do that?

6. Will I also smoke foods?

What's a Grill to Do?

Charcoal grill–A grill that uses charcoal for fuel.

Dual-fuel grills–Some grills now provide the option of cooking with gas and/or other fuels.

Electric grill–An indoor or outdoor grill; heat comes from an electric coil element, so it requires access to an electrical outlet.

Gas grill–An outdoor grill heated by liquid propane (LP) gas or natural gas.

Infrared grill–These grills use infrared radiant energy to produce very high heat very quickly; they also operate with uniform heat, resulting in consistent cooking. These grills are fueled with natural gas or LP gas.

Kamado cooker–Egg-shaped ceramic cookers that are charcoal-fired; they originated in the Far East.

Kettle grill–Round or nearly round charcoal grill with a cover; typically stands on three legs.

Pellet grill–An outdoor grill that uses wood pellets for fuel.

Portable grill–Any grill small and lightweight enough to be carried to a barbecue event; they range from aluminum foil throwaway grills to stainless steel models.

Smoker–Charcoal, wood, a combination of both, electric, or natural gas or LP gas can fuel smoker grills, which are available in numerous configurations.

Turkey fryer–Can be fueled by LP gas or electricity; is filled with oil for frying, or can be used to boil or steam foods.

Source: Hearth, Patio & Barbecue Association

How you answer these questions will help you focus your search on the best grill for you.

Gas grills are popular since they're easy to start and ready to go inside 10 minutes. It's easy to maintain a consistent temperature with gas grills, and if you're using a full-sized propane tank, you don't have to worry much about fuel (a tank will last 20 hours or so).

Gas grills also make it easy to cook at different temperatures at the same time, depending on how many heating elements you have. Be sure to buy one with at least two so you'll be able to use indirect heat for dishes like ribs and beer-butt chicken. Keep in mind, though, that gas grills need a certain amount of flame to stay on, and you won't be able to cook at temperatures lower than

Photo: Jerry Lai

350°–300°F depending on the model you have. More on that when we talk about charcoal and smokers.

When shopping for a portable grill make sure you can get an adapter for full-sized tanks. Most of them use propane cylinders, which don't last as long, and you'll find yourself swapping them out more than you want.

As for what your grill is made of, stainless steel grills are the most durable and least affected by weather. Another benefit of the material is if the cooking grids, burner units, and other parts are stainless steel they won't rust, they'll clean up easily, and they'll last through several football seasons.

Another good choice is cast aluminum grills. These often come with powder-coated finishes. They retain heat better than stainless steel and usually require less clean-up, too.

The same is true for charcoal grills, which also come in powder-coated steel. Charcoal offers the flexibility of really high heat for searing while allowing you to cook low-and-slow for barbeque.

That goes back to the point about gas vs. charcoal for indirect heat and

TOP 5 GRILLS

1. Weber Q: This isn't one grill but a line of grills from Weber that are perfect for tailgaters. The Baby Q (whose real name is the Weber Q 100 series) is an ultra-portable grill with 189 square inches of cooking space and 8,500 BTU. It weighs just 35 pounds and can cook the basics like a champ. The Q 200 series is a step  up in size (280 square inches of cooking space) and power (12,000 BTU) and has an available stand to bring it up to full height. It's portable (42 pounds) but big enough to cook a whole chicken. They use the small propane cylinders, but you can get an adapter for the Q 200 to use full-sized propane tanks.

2. Freedom Grill FG-50: These are cool grills. The primary feature is the swing-away arm that attaches the grill to the hitch of your vehicle so it travels outside the car. That means more room for food, gear, and friends inside. That arm will swing out 180-degrees at your tailgate party so you're not grilling alongside your vehicle melting paint and warming a gas tank. It has 352 square inches of cooking space, 12,000 BTU, and fold-out side tables. You can use  either propane cylinders or full-sized tanks, but you'll need to buy the tank adapter separately. It does come with a 3-year/36,000-mile warranty.

3. Thermos Grill 2 Go: It's a full-sized grill that folds up and rolls like luggage making it a great tailgate grill. Once unfolded and on its legs it stands at normal grilling height (you can also take off the legs for tabletop grilling) and has both a 308-square-inch grill and 140-square-inch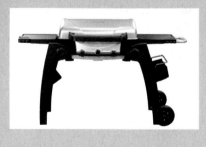

nonstick griddle. The folding side shelves have tool hooks and a car flag holder, there's a grill light that can double as a flashlight, and it has a built-in paper towel holder. It uses propane cylinders, but you can buy an adapter for full-sized tanks.

4. Woodflame Delecto: This isn't your ordinary grill. It's small (just 17 pounds) and uses wood for fuel, and its award-winning design can cook your food at temperatures up to 1,000ºF (it usually takes a 60,000 BTU grill to do that). It burns hardwood cubes and uses a variable speed fan to blow hot air through a system of baffles to the cooking surface. This also does a pretty good job of giving your food smoked flavor. A small amount of wood will get to temperature in just 2 minutes, and the grill fully  cools down in only 15 minutes. Of course, since it uses a fan it needs electricity, but it can run on 4 D-sized batteries, a standard 110-volt outlet, or a 12-volt car adapter. You'll also need a fire starter since you can't use lighter fluid with this grill.

5. Solaire Anywhere Infrared Grill: Solaire makes several high end grills, and this portable has many of the same features but weighs just 20 pounds. These are gas grills, but they use infrared burners to create intense direct heat so you're ready to cook in 3 minutes. Plus, since there's not a heat element that traps grease, drippings don't flare up—they instantly vaporize. This unit has one 14,000 BTU infrared burner and 155 square inches of cooking space. That's not a whole lot of space, but food cooks quickly on an infrared grill. It uses propane  cylinders, but you can buy an adapter for full-sized tanks.

Photo: Ed Rode

barbecue. While gas grills don't cook lower than about 300°F, you can easily cook at 200°–250°F with charcoal, which is optimum for the low-and-slow cooking you need to make great barbecue. Cooking with indirect heat is easy, too; just build your fire on one side of the grill.

If you plan on cooking a lot of barbecue or smoked foods you may want to look at buying a smoker instead, or as a second grill. While some can also be used as a regular grill (although they don't have a lot of cooking space), it's the multilevel, slow cooking abilities that make these so popular.

There are two styles of smokers you most often see at tailgate parties: cylindrical water smokers and horizontal smokers.

The water smokers are a great choice if you're just starting out. They're affordable, easy to use, and versatile. Charcoal is the favorite and most common fuel for smokers for the flavor, but there are gas and electric units that can more easily maintain a consistent temperature. Regardless of the fuel, the use of a water pan placed directly over the heat source means your food will stay moist even after hours and hours of slow cooking.

The most common horizontal smokers, on the other hand, look like two barrels side by side. The smaller one is the firebox where you control how much smoke and hot air it sends into the cooking chamber. You also control how much smoke escapes through a smoke stack attached to the main chamber. These are great units for indirect cooking and a favorite of serious tailgate chefs.

Whichever way you go, be sure the grill or smoker you buy is sturdy, well supported, and doesn't dent if you lean on it. Also check for a good warranty.

Once you've settled on your grill, you need to go shopping for some must-have cooking tools. These are the basics you should toss in a bag or other container and keep with your grill. Then all you have to do is grab it and go.

Tongs are at the top the list, and don't go cheap on these. If they break you're flipping burgers with your hands over a fire. Not a wise choice. Also, don't be tempted by the short ones. While they take up less space in your bag, they don't keep your hands clear of the heat and flare-ups.

Other grill bag essentials are at least two spoons, one slotted, the other not; two spatulas; a couple of forks (and I don't mean the plastic ones you're eating with); a basting brush; a tasting spoon; an instant-read thermometer; and at least two knives.

A couple of notes about those knives. First, they should be sharp. Second, they should be used by only the cook. Don't share knives between the food prep area and the bar. If you're

Photo: David Snodgress

TOP 5 SMOKERS

1. Weber Smokey Mountain Cooker Smoker: This is the most popular, and best, of the inexpensive smokers. If you don't believe me, check out the fan blogs on the Internet. It's a standard vertical water smoker but has two 18.5-inch cooking grates so you have room for everything from turkeys to pork shoulders. The Weber's design and top-and-bottom vent system provides good temperature control for several hours–some of those fan sites say for as long as 20 hours.

2. Brinkmann Smoke 'N Pit Pitmaster: This classically designed horizontal smoker is 19 inches in diameter with a 28-inch shelf and 75 pounds of cooking capacity. You'll be able to put a lot of ribs on that. The offset firebox lets you build up a good fire that will last for a few hours, and the firebox vent to the smoke stack lets you control how much air gets in, and smoke gets out, for temperature control. There are three grill levels, and the cooking chamber can also be used as a direct heat grill for burgers or other tailgate fare.

3. Brinkmann Smoke 'N Grill Gas: This is the most popular of the gas smokers on the market. What makes it popular is you can set it and leave it–it doesn't take any attention unless your gas tank runs out. It has an 18,000 BTU burner and two grill surfaces that will hold 50 pounds of food. You can use it as a grill, too, but there's not surface space to cook a lot. Many barbecue enthusiasts will tell you gas smokers just don't provide the same flavor as charcoal or wood–and I think they're right–but for tailgating convenience there're some benefits to cooking with gas.

4. Bar-B-Chef Charcoal Smoker: This is a standard offset horizontal smoker, and it's a good one. It's also big. It's 767 square inches of cooking surface big. If you choose to use it as a conventional grill, you'll be able to cook burgers for just about everyone in the parking lot. As a smoker it has good temperature control and features to make cooking a bit easier such as a firebox warming tray, a large access door, and a wooden tray/work area in front of the unit.

5. Bradley Smoker (Original): It may look more like a refrigerator than a smoker, but of the electric smoker models this is one of the best and easiest to use. Smoke is created by burning wood discs in the smoke generator. A controlled mechanism handles that for you so you get as much smoke as you want without having to tend a fire. You just set it up and leave it alone. Smoking can't get any easier than that. If you go with this smoker keep in mind it uses Bradley flavor bisquettes you have to buy from them. You can also use this unit to roast foods or as a slow cooker.

cutting limes with the same knife that just cut up that chicken you're going to have cross contamination issues and sick tailgaters. Along the same line have at least two cutting boards—three if you want one for the bar. Use one for raw meat and the second for other foods. It's that cross-contamination thing again.

Include with your cooking tools a pot, a sauce pan, and two skillets or fry pans—an 8-inch and a 12-inch are good choices. Do this even if you don't have a side burner on your grill. Heat is heat whether from a burner or a flame so don't be afraid to use pots and pans on the grill and expand your menu beyond the usual grilled foods.

Round out your kit with a grill brush, a couple of aprons, and plenty of tow-

Photo: Jerry Lai

els. You can't have too many towels, and remember to use a different, clean towel after you've washed up from handling raw meats.

With the basics out of the way you can spend some time thinking about some of the extras that will help you grow from griller to tailgate chef. Although these are not necessities, they will make your day in the parking lot easier and help you impress your friends with your culinary skills.

If you plan on cooking kabobs—a great tailgate dish—then you'll want to get some skewers or a kabob basket. Skewers come in wood and metal. If you use wooden ones, be sure to soak them in water or they'll burn up on the grill. Actually, they may anyway; it's not uncommon for soaking alone not to be enough. To avoid this, wrap the exposed parts of the skewers in foil to prevent flare-ups.

If you want to avoid this issue entirely then you can use metal skewers, but be sure to use a towel or hot pad when taking them off the grill—they get hot.

Kabob baskets are another solution, and they prevent pieces from falling into the fire. You just line up your ingredients, close the lid, and place it on the grill. The ingredients stay in place when flipping, too.

A warming rack or drawer is another useful add-on. It's hard to get your entire meal to be ready at the same time at home, and it can be even harder in a parking lot. These little gems keep things warm while you finish up that final dish. Warming racks come standard with some grills, but you can get a variety of styles as accessories. For the warming drawer you'll need to buy a higher-end unit that comes with one.

There are also a lot of nifty gadgets and accessories to help you expand your tailgate menu and feed more people. Some good options:

- If you want to cook anything from a Philly Cheesesteak to bacon and eggs on your grill, the Griddle-Q will let you do it. This restaurant-style griddle fits over the grids of your gas grill.

- A steamer unit will help you tailgate light and healthier and is perfect for vegetables and other sides.

- A Dutch oven expands your vegetable options, too, as well as braised foods, cornbread, cobblers, and more.

- A grill rack lets you cook several racks of ribs at once by standing them on their sides.

Photo: Hanna van Zutphen-Kann

TOP 5 COOLERS

1. Rubbermaid 5-Day Endurance Cooler: Rubbermaid calls this cooler the 5-Day Endurance Cooler because it guarantees it will keep ice for five days at 90°F. That's good, but what makes this a great tailgate cooler is the split lid. This serves a couple of purposes for the parking lot. For one, it keeps your drinks cold since you're opening just part of the lid, which helps keep the cold air in the cooler. This is also a great cooler for the cook. If you put a divider in the cooler (you'll need to buy or create one) then you have ready-made,

easy access to raw meats on one side and vegetables or prepared foods on the other. This helps prevent cross contamination and keeps you from being known as the guy who gets all of his friends sick. This wheeled unit also has 1 ½ inch-deep cup holders on the lid which come in handy.

2. Rubbermaid 13.2 Qt. Slim Cooler: This is the trim, slim cousin to the 5-Day Endurance Cooler. It has the same split lid and cup holders but solves a common problem for many tailgaters–not enough room in the truck or back of the SUV for a cooler and all your tailgate gear. At just 6.7 inches wide this hard cooler can easily fit into spaces other coolers simply can't. But don't confuse this with a small, personal cooler; it will hold 12 12-ounce cans plus ice and a

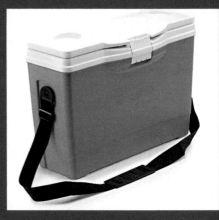

1.5-liter bottle will fit standing upright. It comes with a padded strap in case you have to carry it to your tailgate space.

3. Igloo Cool Fusion 40 Icy Tunes: This cooler and a grill could be all you need to throw your tailgate party. Igloo's Icy Tunes model has speakers and an amplifier, and you can hookup any MP3 player to it. No more running down your car battery. The music player pouch is removable if you want to take your tunes with you as you visit other tailgaters. This 40-quart, wheeled cooler has drink holders built in and external storage. It can also hold up to 58 12-ounce cans and ice.

4. California Innovations All Terrain Rolling Cooler: This cooler is easy to store—it collapses and folds up—and opens up into a rolling cooler with a main compartment that can hold up to 50 12-ounce cans. It also has an "easy access" pocket on the lid so you can reach in and grab a drink without opening up the lid and letting the cold air out. The cooler comes with two cargo pockets for other tailgate supplies.

5. WAECO CoolFreeze: This more than a cooler—it's a portable cooling unit with a compressor that allows you to keep the temperature exactly where you want it—presuming you want it between 0° and 50°F. What that means is it's basically a portable refrigerator. You use an LED touchpad to set the temperature you want and the CoolFreeze will hold the temperature and remember it if the cooler is turned off. It runs on 12/24 volts DC and 110 volts DC and comes in several sizes. These are top-end units with top-end prices so don't be surprised when you see the price tag.

Photo: Ed Rode

- Shaker baskets, fish baskets, and similar styles let you cook small and delicate foods without the fear of them dropping into the fire.
- Grilling lights can be a great help in seeing what you're cooking during night game tailgating.
- Poultry stands, also called chicken racks, make cooking beer-butt chicken and similar dishes much easier.
- If you don't feel like cleaning your grill grates you can get disposable, aluminum grate covers from Clean BBQ, which make clean up as easy as tossing them in the trash.

One last accessory that allows for an impressive tailgate menu is a rotisserie. You can cook any number of things on a rotisserie, but chicken is a popular tailgate choice. But a rotisserie necessitates another discussion—the generator.

Unless you want to stand by your grill turning a hand-crank version for an hour or so, you'll want to have a motorized model and that means electricity. Before buying a generator think about how much stuff you want to power. Honda makes a great little tailgate generator, the EU1000i, that's light (29 pounds) and runs about 8 hours on a tank of gas. It's quiet and is plenty of power for your rotisserie, a TV, radio, fan, blenders, etc.

Of course, your tailgate party needs more than stuff to cook with. You need storage, places to sit, and shelter.

Your primary storage is, of course, the cooler. What type of cooler you get depends on space in the car and how much food and drinks you want to have. A good rule of thumb is get as big or as many coolers as you can take with you. You will find things to fill them up, trust me. If at all possible take at least two coolers so you can pack raw meats and similar items in one and the rest of your food and drinks in the other to avoid cross contamination.

It's also best to pack your coolers with ice blocks or ice packs of some sort rather than loose ice. Why? Because loose ice melts faster. One trick many tailgaters use is to fill an empty milk jug with water and freeze it. On game day it serves as an ice pack for the cooler and once the ice does melt you have drinking water.

When packing your cooler, pre-cool drinks and other items before packing and load the cooler as full as possible; it stays colder longer full than partially filled.

You can also use your coolers to keep hot foods warm. Insulation works both ways, after all. For best results line the cooler with towels, place the warmed dishes on them, and then fill up the rest of the cooler with more towels so you don't have empty space inside.

Tables are another essential for your parking lot party, and one is not enough. The cook should have his own table, and you can never have too much flat space for your buffet and bar. Make sure all of your tables have locking mechanisms for the legs so they don't collapse from the weight of your food or your buddy Paul, who decides to impress your guests with his table dance.

If you have an unused hitch on your vehicle, you can attach a Sports Fan Tailgate Table to it for table space. This handy table attaches to the hitch of your vehicle and travels locked-down outside. At your tailgate party you can set it up for dining or bar height.

TOP 5 CHAIRS

1. Take-a-Seat: It got its national debut on ABC's *American Inventor* as a 3-in-1 tool for tailgaters and bicyclists. The Take-a-Seat attaches to your vehicle's hitch, which leaves more room inside for other gear. At the game you open it up and it unfolds into a two-seat bench. The metal frame is also sturdy enough to use as a frame for carrying gear and is designed to also be a bike rack.

2. Hammaka Sports Chair: This is another hitch-mounted chair, but it supports a hammock-style chair that hangs behind your vehicle. The chair sports an inflatable pillow and footrest, as well as a drink holder. There's also a tripod mount available, which allows you to use the Hammaka Sports Chair without a trailer hitch.

3. Insta-bench: It may fold up into a carrying case and weigh just 20 pounds, but the Insta-bench unfolds to create bench seating for up to six people who weigh up to 1,500 pounds. Okay, not each, but each bench seat holds up to 250 pounds and can be used anywhere. There's also a three-seat version if you have a smaller tailgate crowd.

Fold-away picnic table sets are a great option, too, because they're portable and take care of both table and seating issues.

Seating is something else it's hard to have too much of. While tailgate parties are not usually sit-down dinners, your guests will be hanging out for a while and will want to take a load off. You can use anything from camp stools

4. Tailgate Chair with Side Table: This collapsible chair offers seating and a place to put your food or drink. In addition to the side table, the chair has three pouches that can fit anything from your keys or mobile phone to a newspaper or game-day program.

5. Texsport Folding Picnic Table with Umbrella
This cleverly designed table set travels in a compact case, but when you open it up you have plenty of space to seat four and the umbrella fits in the middle to keep you shaded if you don't have a tent. The table/seat frame is made of durable aluminum and steel and opens to a table top size of 33.5 x 25.5 inches. The umbrella opens to 56 inches. It's designed for camping but works great in the parking lot, too.

and collapsible chairs to new items like fold-out benches and seats that attach to the hitch of your vehicle.

Shelter is another good thing to have at your tailgate party. In addition to providing shade from the sun and dryness from the rain, it helps put a structure to your tailgate space. They're also great for attaching decorations, flags, and other items that create a festive atmosphere and make your tailgate stand out in the parking lot.

Probably the most popular tent at tailgate parties across the country is the E-Z UP Instant Shelter. They take just a few seconds to set up and come in a number of sizes, although their best-selling tent is the 10 x 10 foot model. For a few extra bucks you can add sides, screens, even rain gutters.

The Tailgate Bar
If the grill is the main character of the tailgate party, then the bar is the

supporting actor. It can be as basic as a single cooler. It can be as complex as a nightclub. But it has to be there.

The bar setup begins at home. Take a look at your guest list and determine what you really need to take. Soft drinks and beer may be all you need. Or your old college buddies may demand microbrews and a full bar. If you're throwing a themed tailgate you may have special needs. Frozen margaritas anyone?

Aside from the drinks themselves, there are three things every tailgate bar needs: tables, coolers, and ice.

Just like for the cook and the buffet, you can't have too much table space for the bar. Your bar table needs to be big enough for the bartender to do his thing and for your guests to set down their plates and cups while getting a beer from the cooler.

As for coolers, you want to have at least one dedicated to the bar. This is both for food safety and for convenience. Set the cooler on the opposite end of the table from where you have the staging area for cocktails and wine so you don't have people mowing down each other trying to get a drink.

Photo: JC Ridley

What you add to these basic elements is a direct result of what your guests need or how much you want to show off. Here's a list of items that make up the ultimate tailgate bar; you can pick and choose what's going to take care of your tailgating pals.

- **Bar caddie (the kind that hold garnishes, not the kind that looks for your golf ball while you're at the bar)**
- **Bar/drink mat**
- **Bar towels**
- **Blender**
- **Bottle opener**
- **Cork screw**
- **Jigger/shot glass**
- **Knife and cutting board (each dedicated to the bar—no sharing with the cook)**
- **Mixed drink guide**
- **Napkins**
- **Shaker**
- **Strainer**
- **Swizzle sticks/stirrers**
- **Trash can (dedicated to the bar)**
- **Wine cooler (I'm talking about the bucket for white wine, not the drink.)**
- **Wine glasses, cups, tumblers, etc. (plastic ones are fine for tailgating and make for much easier cleanup and less broken glass)**

And don't forget to serve responsibly. You want to make sure your friends get home safely.

Top 5 Tailgate Toys

1. Cruzin Cooler: Their slogan is "Cool, Very Cool," and it is. This motorized cooler will carry you around the parking lot at up to 13 miles an hour and keep your drinks cold. You can get your cooler in gas and electric models—gas coolers have a 30 mile range, electric ones only 10. Even with the motor inside, the cooler has room for more than 24 cans and ice. If you need more room you can tow the Cruzin Cooler Wagon behind you. On top there are cup holders in the lid.

2. Tailgator Gas Powered Blender: Not a lot of blenders come with a 2-stroke engine, but this one does. That means you don't need electricity, and you can have your margaritas ready in about 15 seconds. At 10 pounds it's a great, portable tailgate blender that will blow your bar menu options wide open. An optional carrying case/backpack has room for the blender, liquor, and mixers.

3. The Wave Box: Now you can be in the parking lot and warm up food, reheat a drink, or pop popcorn in a microwave just like at home. Well, not just like at home—it is much smaller at 10 x 7 x 6 inches inside—but it is the first truly portable microwave. It hooks up to AC and DC, the latter either with a ciga-rette lighter adapter or directly to your car battery. It weighs 14 pounds and has a carrying handle attached.

4. The Beer Belly: This neoprene sling and polyurethane bladder will make you look like you've had plenty of beer in your life. That's your cover. It's designed to conceal beer or other beverages from detection when you head to your seats. Just slip it on, put a shirt on over it, and you have six-pack abs . . . literally. It holds 80 ounces, which if you do the math is 6 1/2 beers. There's a tube you can run out of your collar or sleeve to enjoy your beverage. While it looks like a gut on men, on women you'll look a few months pregnant. Still a good cover.

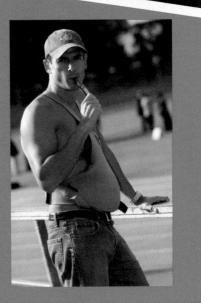

5. Sippin' Seat: It's a seat cushion with a secret. On the outside it looks like one of any number of cushions you can buy to make sitting on the bleachers more comfortable, but inside it has what they call an "internal flexible flask" that holds three cans of beer or whatever else you're drinking. It's another way to slip a beverage inside, although you'll find several Sippin' Seats in the tailgate lot, too.

Tailgate Safety

Tailgating is fun, but accidents do happen. After all, you're using fire, knives, and alcohol. You're sitting for hours in the heat–or cold. While you don't need to be thinking about injuries while enjoying your tailgate party, you should think about them before you head to the parking lot.

A first-aid kit is just as important for your tailgate party as a grill and cooler. Pack it at the beginning of the season, put it in you car or tailgating bag, and don't bother yourself with it again–but it will be there when you need it.

The cell phone is what you'll probably reach for first when there's an emergency, but even for relatively minor accidents you'll need to do something to help the injured between the time you dial and the time professional help arrives. The items on this list will help you do that.

- Adhesive bandages
- Alcohol swabs/antiseptic wipes
- Antacids
- Aspirin
- Blanket (if not in your first-aid kit, at least nearby)
- Burn creams (including sun burn creams)
- Disposable instant cold pack
- Elastic bandages (for wrapping sprained ankles, etc.)
- First-aid tape
- Hydrocortisone cream
- Ibuprofen or acetaminophen
- Plastic/latex gloves
- Scissors
- Sterile gauze pads
- Thermometer
- Triple antibiotic ointment
- Tweezers

Make sure to include in your first-aid kit a list of emergency phone numbers for the area where you're tailgating. You know 911 for major, life-threatening emergencies, but also include the nonemergency phone numbers for the police and fire departments, as well as the numbers for poison control and other similar organizations.

FANATIC FANS

WEIRDWOLF

Take a look at Kansas City Chiefs super fan Weirdwolf's picture and answer this question:

This man is _____ .

A. Part of a prominent Kansas City family

B. From a Mennonite dairy farm

C. An animal handler at the Kansas City Zoo

The answer is "B." I'm not making that up.

Lynn Schmidt was born and raised on a Mennonite dairy farm in Kansas. But his family was progressive, and he got to watch TV as a child. That's why by age 11 he had become a Chiefs fan. That was 1971.

Fast forward to the mid-1990s. Lynn had moved around a bit but settled in the Kansas City area and got to attend his first game in person. That was the start of his transformation from human to Weirdwolf.

While it would be great for the story to include full moons, potions, and rituals with wild wolves, the real story takes shape in a Goodwill store. That's where one day Lynn found a set of football pads and bought them. He took the pads home and painted them the Chiefs' colors. Then he added pieces to them . . . and then to himself. After a while he looked like a juiced-up version of his fanatic fan mentor, Krazy George, who had cheered in KC when Lynn was younger.

But he didn't have a name.

For that, he dipped back in history to The Wolfpack of the Chiefs' first home, Municipal Stadium. The Wolfpack was a group of rowdy fans who sat in the bleachers behind the home team. He decided The Wolfpack would reappear at Arrowhead in the form of Weirdwolf. It's worked. Many fans know him by sight better than they know the players.

"I'm a celebrity among a select group of 80,000," Lynn modestly says. He's more like a rock star.

As soon as he steps out of his car in the parking lot, everyone with a camera comes over for a picture. He signs some autographs as he works his way to his seat. And if he's lucky he gets to cheer and watch some of the game between requests for more pictures. But he doesn't mind because he gets the crowd engaged in the game this way. "That's how I can affect what happens on the field," he says. "The fans help change the outcome of the game."

He's also helped change the outcome of scores of lives with his organization of the KC Superfans—a group comprised of Weirdwolf and several other fanatical Chiefs fans who attend games in face paint and get-ups. The group is modeled after Washington Redskins fans The Hogettes and throughout the year the Superfans raise money for Kansas City charities.

All of this has not gone unnoticed by the Chiefs and the NFL. In 2002 Weirdwolf was inducted into the Pro Football Hall Of Fame VISA Hall of Fans.

WHODEY BABY

The guy in the big striped hat was hooked when his team switched to smaller striped hats.

It was the 1981 season when the Cincinnati Bengals first took the field in

their new, striped helmets. Six-year-old Shawn Moore thought they were way cooler than the old helmets with "BENGALS" spelled out on them. That's when Shawn became a fan.

But it would be another 18 years before Shawn became *the* fan.

In the 1990s Shawn began to upgrade his game-day wardrobe for Bengals games. But it was 1999 when a lime green, souvenir foam hat from Sea World turned Shawn into Whodey Baby.

He saw the hat sitting in his room and decided to paint it orange and black to look like the Bengals helmets. He added to it the face paint and some other accessories and a legend was born (he was inducted into the Pro Football Hall of Fame VISA Hall of Fans in 2003).

"I don't know why I did it, I just did it," Shawn says. "It's the ultimate way to express your support."

And he's been doing that for years—including the down years when Cincinnati was eliminated from playoff contention during the preseason. Okay, it only seemed that way, but Whodey Baby took a lot of heat then. He gets a lot of high fives now. Both for the team's success and his outfit.

He spends his Sundays at Paul Brown Stadium handing out his trading cards, signing autographs, and posing for photos. He's also asked to show off his Bengals tattoo. Believe it or not, it was a gift from his wife.

So what's next for Whodey Baby? Well, this season Shawn says he's glamming it up and going Hollywood. The hat will get a new paint job, and he'll probably update his shoes, and continue to keep Whodey Baby current. After all, he has to be there for his team. That's the whole point.

"Stick with your team no matter what—and show it. This is my way to show it."

SPIKING VIKING

Patrick Olsen is a lifelong Minnesota Vikings fan. But he had always been your run-of-the-mill fan. Loyal, but nothing out of the ordinary.

Patrick, however, was a little out of the ordinary; unless your definition of ordinary includes having a black and red, spiked Mohawk. (The look works with his gig as a hard rock DJ.)

One day the two worlds collided.

He didn't have a chance to go to games growing up, but he did get to go to the 1999 game when the Green Bay Packers came to town. He decided to dye his Mohawk purple and gold to support his Vikings against the hated Packers.

In the "better to be lucky than good" category, a liquor company was holding a crazy fan contest at the game and picked Patrick out of the crowd as a finalist. And he won. His prize was a trip to the Super Bowl. That's when he told himself, "Hey, I'm on to something."

So he added to his look with face paint (in his case face-and-head paint), a

Photo: Fanatical

custom, Spiking Viking jersey, and some beads. He quickly became a Minnesota celebrity. "When I started there weren't a lot of crazy guys around doing this," he explains, "so I just went along for the ride."

It's been quite a ride. He's been inducted into the Pro Football Hall of Fame VISA Hall of Fans, he's been on TV shows, and the Vikings use him to help pitch season tickets in the game program.

For Patrick game day starts during the week when he touches up his dye job. On Sunday he's up at 6 a.m. to start the spiking process, which includes an ample supply of instant freeze hair spray. That takes about 30 minutes. Then the jersey goes on, and he sits down for another 20–30 minutes to apply his face paint. Then he gathers his tailgating supplies and heads to the stadium.

That's when his day gets crazy. He can't walk 5 feet without someone stopping him to take a picture. Those people are usually adults. "Kids get a little scared of me," Patrick says.

"I never dreamed of doing this for the celebrity, it was just to have fun. But I know that's a part of it, and it adds to the game-day atmosphere for fans. I want people to say 'Yeah, he's crazy, but even if the game stunk I still had fun, and he made me laugh.'"

He'll be doing that in a different uniform this season. The Vikings have new uniforms so he'll update his, too. He'll also change his number from 11 (since Dante Culpepper is gone) to 12 (for the 12th man). As a final touch he plans to make that famous Mohawk purple and gold.

And to answer the question you've had since you first saw the photo of the purple hair, it's naturally brown.

BOSS HOGETTE

So what inspires a grown man to put on a dress and a pig nose? His grandmother.

It was 1983, and the retirement home where Mike Torbert's

grandmother lived held a Halloween Tacky Tea Party. He borrowed her black-and-white polka-dot dress and surprised her. He was a hit, and Mikey T. Boss Hogette was born. But there's more to the story.

Mike is a Washington Redskins fan, and at the time of his transformation the offensive line was known as The Hogs and was credited with making much of the team's success possible (the Skins played in the Super Bowl in 1983 and 1984). Mike felt the Hogs needed a cheerleading squad, so he recruited a dozen friends to don dresses, pig noses, wigs, and "good guy" leather hats to create that squad: The Hogettes.

He did all of this for fun and to have a hook to help raise money for children's charities in the area. But it wouldn't take long for him to realize this would be more than just some guys having fun in women's clothing.

"I got a pretty good indication the very first game we went to in 1983," Mike recalls. "One of our first guys was a retired navy chief and he's a big guy, and pretty ugly, but this guy from *USA Today* must have taken two rolls of film of this guy's face. So I knew right away this had something to it."

Before we get to what that "something" turned out to be, it's interesting to know that these guys are not your stereotypical wacky fans, or guys who spent more time with a keg than a textbook in college. Mike is nuclear waste engineer for the Department of Energy. Other Hogettes include retired navy officers, a navy SEAL, and the guy who ran the Pentagon's spying operation—these are smart guys. And they're all family guys. This isn't anything people expected them to do.

"My wife's very conservative and she couldn't believe I was doing it at first," says Mike. "Once she found out why, she was very supportive."

That's a good thing, because during the past 25 years The Hogettes have become bigger than anyone could have imagined. They've been in commercials for VISA, The Home Depot, and Coke. They've sat on the couch and chatted with Jay Leno. And each year they make more than 100 charity appearances and have helped raise more than $100 million.

"I like to think of us as communicators," Mike explains. "You can spread a laugh pretty quickly when TV hits you for a couple of minutes. That's what we try to do—make people laugh. Especially when you're working with kids that are hurting; it helps a lot."

Today there are 12 active members and 15 "missing links" in The Hogettes, who were inducted into the Pro Football Hall of Fame VISA Hall of Fans when it opened in 1998. On game days you can find them at FedEx Field hosting a big tailgate party with plenty of food ("We eat too much, but we have a reputation to keep up after all.") and plenty of fans wanting pictures with them—Redskins' and opponents'.

He also found a fan at an event in New York's Times Square: Anna Nicole Smith. "She said, 'Take a picture with the pig man.'" And he obliged.

THE PACKALOPE

The Packalope is a product of a passion for the Green Bay Packers, a deer rack, and *America's Funniest Home Videos.* I'll explain.

Larry Primeau is a life-long Packer fan. He came by it naturally-–his father was a huge fan—and in 1973 Larry went to his first game. He's missed very, very few home games in the 3 decades since.

But it was in 1990 when Larry Primeau the fan became Larry Primeau the Packalope. That was when he attached a 6-point deer rack to his

vintage 1960s Packer helmet to wear to the game (he's since upgraded to a 10-point rack). "Don't ask me why I did it," Larry says. "I just did it."

At about the same time his wife was watching *America's Funniest Home Videos* and saw a clip that featured a mythical animal that was half jackrabbit and half antelope–a jackalope. Inspiration struck, and she suggested Larry's game-day alter ego be named the Packalope.

The Packalope was an immediate hit and in the years since has become a Green Bay legend. "You'd think I'd be in everybody's photo album across the country as many pictures as people take," he muses. (He's also become an NFL legend –he was inducted into the Pro Football Hall of Fame VISA Hall of Fans.)

As the legend's grown so has the game-day getup. He's added to the outfit with Packer pants, green and gold shoes, and beads–and he now wears a #47 jersey in honor of his wife who passed away in 2004 at the age of 47. Larry credits her support with inspiring him to create his Packers van, which comes complete with a Packer paint job, green and gold lights, a mural of Lambeau Field inside, and a cheese wedge on top.

He decided to add the cheese wedge since he'd never seen one on a car before. His wife basically said, "Yeah, right." So he took a cheese head, headed to the garage, and replicated it to scale out of plywood (he's a mechanical engineer, so that helped) and painted it. After a few years the weather took its toll, and the van now sports a fiberglass version he had made.

"You know, people come up to me and say, 'You're the #1 fan.' I tell them I'm not the #1 fan; I'm a fan just like you are. I just stand out a little bit more."

THE ULTIMATE STEELERS FAN

Nearly 30 years ago Bud Recktenwald went to his first Pittsburgh Steelers tailgate party. The Iron City native had been a Steelers fan his entire life, so he wanted to make sure he wore his colors to his friend's parking lot party.

Bud wore black and gold and donned his Terrible Towel. Once he got to the stadium, he bought a hat with clapping hands on it from a guy selling them in the parking lot. He knew he was supporting his Steelers and having fun. He didn't know he was about to become a Pittsburgh legend.

A radio reporter saw Bud—the hat was hard to miss—and interviewed him. As he wrapped up the interview, he called Bud "The Ultimate Steelers Fan" and suggested to his audience that everyone should support their team the way Bud does.

"Then it just blossomed into all different kinds of things," Bud recalls. He became a regular at Steelers tailgates, hooking up with other fans like Bob

Garritano (aka "The Terrible Fan"), and participated in pep rallies held by local companies and charities. Others started calling Bud "The Ultimate Steelers Fan," and that's how he's been known ever since.

He's added to the outfit over the years, picking up items here and there or receiving them as gifts. His signature sunglasses came from a visit to a flea market. "When I first went to the tailgating thing, I just had to have my black and gold on," he says. "So I black and gold myself the best I know how." Now everything he wears is black and gold (yes, that includes his Steelers underwear).

He also drives a black and gold van loaded with Steelers memorabilia. He calls it "The Littlest Steeler Van," a nod to his first decked-out car, "The Littlest Steeler," which is now in the Western Pennsylvania Sports Museum. Bud himself is in a different museum, enshrined in the Pro Football Hall of Fame VISA Hall of Fans.

Bud will tell you all of the recognition is great, but he's always done this for fun and to make other people smile. "I'm here for people to laugh at me and bring a smile to their face before the game," he explains.

"Everybody comes over and takes pictures and I get all kinds of hugs. When I go into a game I get *guys* hugging me saying, 'You're the best!' I say, 'Thanks, but you're not getting my Bud Light!'"

PLANNING YOUR TAILGATE PARTY

The Setup

The explorer Roald Amundsen said, "Adventure is just bad planning." Tailgating isn't supposed to be an adventure. It's supposed to be fun.

That's why you need to spend some time before game day planning for what you need and how you'll set up your tailgate party. That includes everything from what you're serving to how many chairs you'll need to how you're going to pack it in your vehicle.

The best way to do this is with a checklist. I guarantee you Roald Amundsen used one; you should, too. In the parking lot you don't have your kitchen nearby to grab stuff your forgot, and, unless you want to lose your tailgate space and watch the game on TV somewhere, you're not going to be able to make a quick run to Wal-Mart, either.

Photo: Luke Adams

The list below will get you started. It may be most everything you need, but walk through your tailgate party and add to the list everything you can think of. Don't forget the ingredients to your menu. It's easier than you think to forget something as simple as salt, or as critical to your friends' happiness as the beer.

A lot of tailgaters will make their list at the beginning of the season, laminate it, and attach it to their cooler or other tailgate container. Then they use a grease pencil to check off items as they pack them. After the game they wipe the list clean and it's ready for the next game. It's a good system.

The Ultimate Tailgater's Checklist

FOR YOUR VEHICLE

Your best bet is to put a vehicle kit together at the beginning of the season with these items and keep it in your vehicle or somewhere handy to grab on your way to the game.

- Blankets
- De-icer
- First-aid kit (see page 27)
- Fix-a-Flat (or similar brand)
- Flares
- Jumper cables
- Map(s)
- Rags
- Water
- Wiper fluid

FOR YOUR TAILGATE SITE

These are the basics you should make sure you have. Add to the list specific items you need for your tailgate party. And when you're packing your car, load in what you'll need last first, and what you'll need as soon as you get to the parking lot last. This way your setup will go more smoothly.

- Antibacterial soap
- Tent/canopy
- Tables
- Chairs
- Decorations
- First-aid kit
- Flashlight
- Insect repellant
- Matches
- Moist towelettes
- Paper towels
- Rope
- Sunscreen
- Trash bags
- Trash cans
- Umbrella

FOR COOKING AND EATING

- Aluminum foil
- Apron
- Ash container
- Bottle opener
- Can opener
- Cleaning supplies
- Coolers
- Cutting boards
- Dishwashing liquid
- Food/spices
- Food storage containers
- Grill/smoker/stovetop
- Ice

Top 3 Tailgating Tips

1. Use a checklist. No one wants to be the guy who has to eat the burger off of the asphalt because someone forgot a plate. I know you think you'll remember everything–after all you do this just about every week–but I guarantee you, you'll forget something. It may be that plate or barbecue sauce or the corkscrew, but it will be something. And your buddies will never let you live it down. So write down everything you'll need, including your menu ingredients, and check them off as you pack up.

2. Prep ahead. Do as much preparation as possible in the days before the game. The whole point of your tailgate party is to have time to spend with your friends and to have fun, so dice the peppers and season the chicken the day before and store them in a zip-top bag or other container so they're ready to use as soon as you're in the parking lot.

3. Ice. Lots of ice. Think you have enough? Get a couple more bags. If there's one common error in parking lots across the country its tailgaters not bringing enough ice. It's frustrating at best, dangerous at worst. You need to keep raw meats and other perishable foods at 40°F or colder, and if you don't have enough ice you can't do that.

- Knives
- Measuring cups/spoons
- Plates/bowls/cups
- Propane or charcoal
- Potholder
- Pots and pans
- Serving dishes
- Serving spoons/forks
- Spatulas
- Tongs
- Towels (cloth and paper)
- Utensils
- Zip-top bags

Tailgate Flow Triangle

It doesn't matter how big your tailgate is, it has to have a flow. Whether you're hosting 5 or 50 it's important to set up your space with a flow triangle so everyone can enjoy themselves.

This starts with the grill. It needs to be set outside your main tailgate area, not under the tent (unless you like sitting in smoke). Next to the grill place a work table, cooler space, and a trash can. This is where the tailgate chef will spend a good part of the day, and you don't want to crowd the cook.

The second point on the triangle is your buffet table. If you have a tent it should be under it and have enough space to lay out your food while allowing guests to move around it comfortably. Hungry people can get grumpy, and no one wants to see anyone shoving aside your great aunt on the way to the brats.

The third point on the triangle is the bar. It should be away from the buffet and have its own table, cooler, and trash can. This way people can easily get their drinks and socialize without being in the way of the rest of the party.

Your conversation area goes in the center of your flow triangle with plenty of chairs and space for people to socialize.

TRICKED-OUT TAILGATES

THE BIG G

It started with a high school road trip to Tampa Bay. Stephen Gay and some of his buddies headed south to see their Green Bay Packers take on the Buccaneers. They rented an RV and hit the road.

Along the way they talked about how they all should chip in and buy their own RV and turn it into a party vehicle. It was a great idea.

But it never happened.

Instead, Stephen's friends lost that ambition. So Stephen went RV shopping alone, and in 1993 bought a 1966 Dodge Travco Motorhome. It wasn't in the best of shape, but it seemed cosmically ordained he should buy it. It was a 1966 model. Stephen's favorite Packer was Ray Nitschke who wore the number 66. The Packers' first Super Bowl season was 1966. He couldn't say no.

He also couldn't leave it alone. Right away he looked at his new vehicle and told himself, "That could be a helmet." So he painted a two-dimensional Green Bay hel-met on it. But he's not an artist, and the design wasn't symmetrically correct and just didn't look right.

Sara Schaller is an artist and a friend of Stephen's. So for

the 1994 season she agreed to repaint what Stephen now called The Big G with a symmetrically correct, 3-D helmet. As soon as Stephen rolled his newly renovated RV into the parking lot people went nuts.

"No one who has a camera walks by without stopping to take a picture of The Big G," Stephen says. And during the next decade Stephen became a parking lot celebrity. Well, The Big G has.

It's been featured in an NFL Films story about Super Bowl XXXII, when the Packers lost to the Denver Broncos in San Diego. It was the backdrop for a Campbell's Soup commercial. It's been featured in a number of news features.

Ironically, Stephen hasn't asked for any of this. He's never sought publicity. He just did this to have fun. The Big G itself has attracted more attention than he ever could imagine.

And on game day it attracts a lot of attention, of course. Stephen throws an open tailgate party each home game, and he loses count of how many people come by to take a picture and peek inside. Not surprisingly, the inside is decked-out in Packer memorabilia.

It's the game-day attention Stephen cherishes. "The special part of it," he explains, "is all of the people I've met from throughout the world who have come by."

Stephen's tried to retire The Big G several times. "But like Brett Favre I just can't seem to do it," Stephen says. So he's still nursing the RV, which has been stuck on 19,999 miles for years and has no gas gauge (he just knows to fill it up every 250 miles). It isn't cheap ("I couldn't put a number on it; if I did I'd cry."), but the tailgate parties are worth it.

And for Stephen that's what it's all about. He never goes inside the stadium. He watches the game on one of The Big G's TVs, playing host to his guests.

So if you're in Green Bay for a game head over to the old West Side Godfather's Pizza site on Ridge Road and join the party. If you want to meet Stephen, look for the guy in shorts and a T-shirt. Even in December. Even in the snow.

"I've never worn anything else to a game," he'll tell you. "I started when I was young and kept it going."

Good thing The Big G has heat.

OSU SCHOOL BUS

Ted Kuhn's been an Ohio State fan for years. His son played in the band. He's been to a lot of games and has seen a lot of converted school buses in the tailgate lots.

In 2004 he decided he needed one of his own. Timing is everything, and just as he started looking, some students who had been in the band with his son decided to sell their party bus. It was a mess—they're college kids, after all—but it was mechanically in great shape so he bought it and drove it to his Dublin, Ohio, home.

That's where over six months (mostly during weekends) the transformation took place that created the OSU School Bus.

The outside sports murals of the OSU band—a tribute to both the school and his son. The inside is a rolling diner and unlike any school bus you've ever seen.

Along one side of the bus is an antique soda fountain. Along the other is an original wooden bench from C Deck of the old OSU stadium; it was a gift from his son and still has the original numbering and some gum stuck underneath. Both sit on a checker board floor that takes you back to the 1950s. To top it off is a soda fountain table and stools, Buckeye souvenirs and memorabilia, and three TVs with satellite service. Three golf cart batteries keep everything running.

The bus is a well-known game-day attraction outside Ohio Stadium and was the catalyst to forming the OSU School Bus Tailgaters club. The club has a couple dozen members from around the state that meet at the games and tailgate together. The club has officers, a newsletter, and a Web site (osuschoolbustailgaters.com).

If you want to join you have to have a school bus, pay $30 a year for dues, and be ultimate tailgaters. "We get to the stadium about 6:30 in the morning no matter what time the game is," Ted explains. "We have breakfast and lunch, and tailgate until game time. Some of us go into the game and a lot stay on the bus and watch it there."

"Except for the Michigan game; we get there at 4:30 in the morning then."

THE FANBULANCE

Its first life was running calls across Iowa. Once it was retired from active duty, a "For Sale" sign went up on it.

That's when Tom Dunn became the owner of an ambulance.

He wasn't in need of medical care. Tom and his family are big Atlanta Falcons fans, and the ambulance seemed like the perfect vehicle to customize into a Medi Vick unit for tailgating (get it?). So he hopped on a plane to Iowa and drove it home.

Before the Fanbulance, Tom and his tailgating crew—the BirdWatchers—tailgated out of a van and a Pontiac Aztek. (Incidentally, Tom says for his

money the Aztek is the best mass-produced tailgating vehicle ever.) But with his new ambulance he had visions of the ultimate tailgating vehicle dancing in his head. It was time to get to work.

After a few repairs, removing some unneeded medical and some illegal light equipment (you don't get to run blue lights as a private citizen even if your tailgate party has run out of ice and you're on the way to pick up more), it was off to a painter to turn this ambulance into the Fanbulance.

But the new red-and-white design and Falcons graphics, and working lights and sirens, are just part of the story. While those turn heads—and have on more than one occasion had people coming up to Tom asking for medical help—it's what's inside and how he retrofitted the vehicle that makes this a tailgater's dream.

"We have a Freedom Grill on the outside and a microwave and cooler and everything on the inside," Tom says. In addition the storage compartments on the outside of the box contain chairs, tables, flags, awnings, a generator, and other tailgating gear. Inside, in addition to the microwave and cooler, there's a blender, seating, and other tools for a great tailgate party. The television rotates for viewing from either inside the vehicle or out the back doors. It has 110-power, "so anything you can use at your house we can use at our tailgate party."

The Fanbulance has won awards from folks ranging from Campbell's Soup to Jack Daniels (it's a three-time Jack Daniels tailgate champ) and wins praises from just about everyone who sees it . . . even opposing fans.

If you want to see the Fanbulance visit a Falcons home game this season and amble to the lot across Magnum Street from the southeast corner of the Georgia Dome. Trust me, you won't miss it.

CARNIVORE

First of all, you just gotta love the name.

This tricked-out 2005 Chevrolet Silverado isn't about supporting a team; it's about supporting a killer tailgate party. This truly is a sports bar on wheels.

Steve Glor, who customized his truck into "Carnivore" to show off his company's Freedom Grills, spent a year working with a slew of vendors to turn his 4x4 into what he calls "the last word in tailgating vehicles."

The first thing you notice, of course, is the paint job. The flames and barbecue shadows are designed to "bring out the heat." The light bar and other

external features are eye catching, too. But what draws a crowd is when Steve punches a few buttons and the 4x4 becomes a kitchen, sports bar, and entertainment center all in one.

That button-pushing causes the truck's bed cover to rise up, the bedsides to fold down, and wood counter tops to come out providing a bar around the back for hanging out and watching the flat panel TVs that hang from underneath the bed cover. (There are seven screens on the truck when you add them all up.)

The audio system will rock even the tailgate parties around you, and with the Freedom Grill and other appliances Carnivore provides a portable kitchen and bar that will be the envy of the parking lot. There's even a "Grill Cam" so those sitting in the truck's cab can see what's going on around the bar and grill in back.

"When we have this opened up there isn't anyone who can just walk by it," says Steve. "Everyone comes over to check it out and hang out for a while. We feed a lot of people on game day."

BLUEBIRD

You hear all the time how marriage is compromise. But it usually doesn't include tailgating trucks. But most people aren't Elizabeth and Keith Moodie.

First some background.

He is a die-hard New York Giants fan. She grew up cheering on the Philadelphia Eagles. Both love football and to tailgate. So much so that after their wedding ceremony at a Dave & Buster's (he wore a Giants vest while taking his vows), the two loaded their guests into buses and took them to an Eagles game as their wedding reception.

Knowing that, it may not come as a surprise that as the newlyweds began planning for tailgate parties as a couple they found themselves with more tail-

gate gear than they had space to haul it. So during the 2003 season they bought a plain, white box truck to carry their tailgate supplies. It didn't stay plain or white for long.

They had airbrush artist Art Simpson paint half of the van Giants blue with a huge helmet and "Go Big Blue" on the back. The other half of the van he painted Eagles green with that team's helmet and "Fly Eagles Fly" on the back. Thus, the BlueBird tailgating vehicle came to be.

The couple carried the split-personality inside the bus, which resembles your living room more than a truck, with paneling, carpet, a couch, custom benches, and two TVs.

When they pulled into the parking lot for the first time – at both the Linc and at Giants Stadium—their reception was mixed. If the local fans saw the hometown team side first the Moodies got high fives. If they saw the visiting team side first the hand gestures were different. But Keith says once people saw the other side of the truck they thought it was great, and they've been welcomed in both cities. Even if fans are a bit confused.

"Some people comment on their way into the stadium," he says, "and when they leave they see the other side and they don't even realize it's the same truck."

Of course, the BlueBird has meant minor-celebrity status for the Moodies in Philly and New York. They knew right away they had something popular when at the first game they tailgated with BlueBird they ended up in a commercial for ESPN.

For the past several years the couple has tailgated with the BlueBird in the same lot with the same group of friends at both stadiums—Lot E at the Linc, Lot 8B at Giants Stadium. But that's about to change.

The Moodies are expecting their first child this fall and the BlueBird is a two-seater. The math doesn't work; so they've sold the BlueBird. But the buyers know the vehicle well. They're the Lot 8B Tailgaters at Giants Stadium. "We've kept it in the family," Keith says.

But even that won't mean one of the country's most memorable tailgating vehicles will see another season. Keith says the truck will probably become a Giants/Wildcats truck since many of the Lot 8B Tailgaters are Villanova alumni (hence the Wildcats).

But don't worry about the Moodies or their new child. Keith says they'll have a new tailgating vehicle ready when the season kicks-off and it will have an infant seat. "Our goal," explains Keith "is for our child to never miss a Giants/Eagles game ever."

DIMOZINE

Take a trailer like the ones NASCAR drivers use to haul their cars around the country, turn it into an urban barbecue vehicle that sleeps four, park it outside Reliant Stadium in Houston, and you have the Dimozine (yes, it rhymes with limousine). It's amazing what some margaritas and a bar napkin can create.

That, according to DIM Cookers team members Tad Cook and John Swazey, is how this tricked-out tailgate vehicle came about. "It started off like every project, 'If we're going to do this, why don't we do this? If we're going to do this, why don't we add this?' And the next thing we knew we'd drawn up a 41-foot trailer with sleeping quarters and the pit and the kitchen and everything like that."

The Dimozine has a fire box and two pits—one large, the other smaller—that churn out enough food to feed more than 100 people every game day. There are four catering doors that open up on the sides, and if you walk in the main door you enter a living area with diamond plate flooring, a kitchen, televisions, a bar, a bathroom, and four bunks.

They also use the trailer to compete in barbecue contests when they aren't

tailgating before a Houston Texans game. But they say there's something special about those Texans tailgates. "We all grew up as Oilers fans and at that time you just had to get out of your car and walk into the stadium. You couldn't even have chicken in your car. So everybody in town was looking forward to this tailgating thing."

So do the hundreds of fans who enjoy the barbecue brisket, ribs, chicken, and other dishes DIM Cookers serve up each week.

THE BATTLE WAGON

You won't find many fans more dedicated to their Minnesota Vikings than The Wagoneers. These are the guys who built the Battle Wagon. This is the kind of wagon you want to go into battle with. Well, at least to hang out in before the battle.

The inspiration came one day in 1998 when the group of friends was huddled around a fire in a parking lot trying to stay warm before a Vikings game. Maybe it was the beer. Maybe it was the cold. But the talk turned to how other tailgaters were staying warm in their RVs and trucks. They needed one of those. But they needed more than just a vehicle to keep warm. They needed a Vikings party vehicle.

The guys bought their 1966 Chevy step van from, of all places, a furniture store for $900. Then they started putting more money into it to outfit it into an ultimate tailgating vehicle. How much? They don't know; they haven't kept track. "If nobody knows then our wives can't find out," explains Wagoneer Terry Moravec.

The expenses started piling up right away. After the first game they blew the engine and it had to be replaced. The closest the mechanic could find that would work was a 1972 Nova engine. So they painted it purple and gold and put it in.

Of course, the purple-and-gold theme also covers the outside of the van. It's painted "Ultra Violet," which is a standard color Ford uses and the closest to Viking purple they could find. Tom Griffin—a sign painter and fan—painted the graphics. All-weather speakers on the roof and horns on the hood finish off the look.

The inside of the Battle Wagon is like your den. That's if your den is carpeted in Astroturf. In addition to the turf, they've installed paneled walls, a TV (the satellite dish sits on top of the Battle Wagon), Vikings memorabilia, and a working gas fireplace.

"It's a vent-free propane unit with a heat output of about 28,000 BTUs. That's about 24,000 BTUs more than we need to heat the Battle Wagon," says Terry.

The Battle Wagon first pulled into a tailgate lot in 1999, and since then it has become a local legend and the Wagoneers have become folk heroes, of sorts. That works for them; it means a bigger tailgate party. What could be bad about that?

WHAT TO EAT

Few things draw communities together like food. It's been that way across the globe for generations, and it's no different in the parking lot. Food is the centerpiece of your tailgate party, and it's what your guests will be talking about at work the next week. (Okay, they'll probably talk about the game, too.)

On my show *The Ultimate Tailgater's Podcast*, I get to talk to some of the best chefs in the country about how to create memorable tailgate meals. Some of them are celebrity chefs, others celebrities only in their tailgate lots, but all of them share a passion for food and have great tips and recipes to help you become a better tailgate chef. Many of them offer up some of their dishes on the following pages. I've also included several of my own recipes that have been tailgate party favorites.

For more recipes, podcasts, and videos, log on to theultimatetailgater.com.

RECIPE INDEX

There's a reason they make meat thermometers . . .

It is important to always think about food safety at your tailgate party and thoroughly cook your food. Want to make sure no one comes next week? Serve them undercooked chicken this week. Make sure you have a meat thermometer in your cooking kit, and use it.

RED MEATS

120°F   Rare

125°F   Medium Rare

130°F   Medium

135°F   Medium Well

140°F   Well Done

PORK & VEAL

140°F   Medium

150°F   Well Done

POULTRY

160°F   White Meat Cooked

170°F   Dark Meat Cooked

FISH

120°F   Medium Rare

130°F   Medium/Cooked

NOTE: These fish guidelines are just that. Fish temperatures vary widely so go by firmness, flakiness, and color.

KEVIN ROBERTS, THE FOOD DUDE

You may know Kevin Roberts as radio's The Food Dude, but he's also a chef who likes to tailgate. In his book *Munchies* he has several recipes that are perfect for the parking lot.

For Kevin the key to great meals is to experiment, and don't be afraid to stray from the recipe, although there are a few basics to remember. "The trick is if you're going to do meat, game, that kind of flavor—that kind of protein—you're going to want more robust stuff, the barbecue sauces, the A.1. sauces, the thicker, kind of brown sauces. If you're going to be going chicken or fish you want to go with the light stuff, the lemons, the butters, the white wines . . . you want to keep it light. You're not going to throw A.1. on a piece of red snapper."

Kevin is also a fan of spicing up dishes with hot sauce. But he says that's not the trick to making his popular West Coast Wings. "The trick to my tasty and healthy wings is I boil them first. That knocks off a lot of the fat and makes them nice and tender."

West Coast Wings

THE STEPS

1: Boil the wings in a large pot for 15 minutes. Drain when done.

2: Grill wings on barbecue until crispy.

3: In a large bowl, add the butter and melt in microwave.

4: Add the Frank's Red Hot and mix well.

5: When wings are nice and crispy, add them to the bowl and coat them well.

Serves 4.

INGREDIENTS

1, 4 pound bag of frozen or fresh chicken wings (try to get a combo of both wings and drumettes)

½ stick butter, melted

½–1 bottle Frank's Red Hot Sauce

Recipe © Kevin Roberts, The Food Dude, *Munchies* Cookbook (Storey Publishing, 2004).

RICK BROWNE'S "ORIGINAL BEER-BUTT CHICKEN"

If you want to know about barbecue in America, ask Rick Browne. He hosts the show.

In addition to his PBS series *Barbecue America*, Rick is the author of several barbecue cookbooks and was the first guy to popularize Beer-Butt Chicken. Now it's a favorite of barbecue enthusiasts in parking lots across the country. Rick has spent a lot of time in many of those parking lots. The best tailgate he's experienced was in Kansas City.

"We went to a Chiefs game and . . . we came up the road and came up into the parking lot and I was flabbergasted," Rick recalls. "There was smoke everywhere. It looked like a battlefield from the Civil War. There was so much smoke, and people of every size and description using barbecues of every size and description to barbecue everything from brisket to sausage to burgers to hot dogs to chicken . . . it was unbelievable."

Photo: Milan Chuckovich

If you're one of those people of every size and description, Rick has a tip for you he says far too many tailgaters forget—leave the grill lid closed. You may be proud of those steaks, but every time you open the lid to show them off you lose 15 minutes of cooking time. Check them toward the end of the cooking time with a meat thermometer, but he says to trust yourself and show off your culinary skills with the finished dish.

Beer-Butt Chicken

Mix the rub in a small bowl until it's well incorporated. Wash, dry, and season the chicken generously inside and out with the rub. Work the mixture well into the skin and under the skin wherever possible. Place on a plate, cover, and dry marinate at room temperature for 20 to 30 minutes.

Prepare charcoal or gas barbecue for indirect heating at 375°F.

Pour half the can of beer into a spray bottle, add the cider, olive oil, and balsamic vinegar, and set aside.

Take the (opened) beer can in one hand and insert it into the bird, sliding the chicken tail-side down over the can. This positioning does two things: first it helps drain off the fat as the chicken cooks, second, the beer steams the inside of the chicken, while the outside is cooked by the BBQ heat, making it the most moist bird you've ever laid yer eyes, or gums, on. Some people put a small potato or carrot in the neck opening of the chicken to keep the steam inside; I prefer to let it pass through.

Place in aluminum pie pan with ½ inch water, over high heat for 15 minutes. Spray, then move to a cooler side of the grill for indirect cooking. Cook for 1 ½ to 2 hours over indirect heat,. During the cooking time spray the chicken all around with the basting spray several times. The chicken is done when the internal temperature in the thigh reaches 180°F. After your guests have reacted appropriately, remove the chicken from the beer can with tongs while holding the can with an oven mitt (Careful, that stainless steel is very hot!).

Give the chicken one more spritz of the basting spray and then carve and serve. I love to team up this chicken with buttered noodles, corn bread stuffing, and chilled beer.

Serves 4 to 6.

Recipe compliments of Rick Browne, © 2005 *The Barbecue America Cookbook*

INGREDIENTS:

DRY RUB:

1 teaspoon brown sugar

1 teaspoon garlic powder

1 teaspoon onion powder

1 teaspoon summer savory

¼ teaspoon cayenne pepper

1 teaspoon chili powder

1 teaspoon paprika

1 teaspoon dry yellow mustard

1 tablespoon sea salt

BASTING SPRAY:

1 cup apple cider

2 tablespoons olive oil

2 tablespoons balsamic vinegar

1 cup warm beer

1 12 oz. can of your favorite beer

1 large chicken

Easy Cajun Fried Turkey

Heat peanut oil in large fryer to 350° F.

Dress turkey whole, leaving skin on. Rub thoroughly with Cajun seasoning so all surface area is covered. Lower the turkey into the fryer and cook 3 minutes per pound, plus 5 minutes.

Remove, drain, and let cool before serving.

Serves 4–8.

INGREDIENTS:

1 whole turkey

Cajun seasoning (premixed commercial brands are fine)

Peanut oil

Tip: If you want to try your own Cajun seasoning mix, here's a recipe to get you started. Play with how much of each spice you use until you get a formula you love.

6 parts salt

1 part cayenne

1 part red pepper

1 part pepper

1 part granulated garlic

1 part grated onion

½ part black paprika

Tequila Lime Shrimp

Boil the shrimp, then cool and peel. Mix the other ingredients into a marinade and pour into a zip-top bag with the shrimp. Marinate in the refrigerator for 2 hours.

Serve the shrimp as an appetizer or warm them and use as a taco filling in a corn or flour tortilla. If you choose to use them in tacos, add shredded purple and green cabbage and Pico de Gallo.

Serves 5–6.

INGREDIENTS:

2 pounds medium shrimp

1 shot tequila

1 Jicama, finely chopped

1 bunch cilantro, finely chopped

1 medium yellow onion, finely chopped

½ cup vegetable oil

Juice of 1 lime

Tailgate Tenderloin

In a bowl combine all of the ingredients for the spice rub and mix thoroughly. Rub the mixture on all surfaces of the tenderloins, massaging it into the meat. Let rest 20–30 minutes (or refrigerate as long as overnight).

In another bowl combine the orange juice, garlic, salt, and cayenne and mix. Whisk in the honey, olive oil, and tequila until combined. Set aside for basting.

Preheat grill for indirect cooking with high heat on one side.

Place tenderloins over high heat for 10 minutes, turning 2–3 times and basting with the sauce. Then move the tenderloins to the cool side of the grill and cook for another 15–20 minutes, or until done. During this time turn twice and baste with the sauce.

When done remove from the grill and let rest 10 minutes before slicing and serving.

Serves 8–10.

INGREDIENTS:

4 pork tenderloins (about 1 pound each)

Spice Rub

2 tablespoons paprika

2 tablespoons chili powder

2 tablespoons oregano

2 teaspoons kosher salt

1 teaspoon red pepper flakes

Basting Sauce

1 ½ cups orange juice

2 tablespoons minced garlic

2 teaspoons kosher salt

½ teaspoon cayenne

4 tablespoons honey

2 tablespoons olive oil

1 ½ tablespoons tequila

Photo: Dave Snodgress

KERRY BYRNE'S SMOKY VENISON CHILI

Kerry Byrne lives two lives. During the week he's the food writer for the *Boston Herald* reviewing Michelin 3-Star restaurants and fancy dishes. During the weekend he's the guy who butchers his own pigs and tailgates with the 225 Club—if you don't weigh at least 225 pounds you can't get in. These guys know food and tailgating.

Kerry is a traditionalist in the parking lot, especially when it comes to the grill. "My pet peeve is propane," he says. "I think propane is an affront to the gridiron gods. Food never tastes as good on propane. I know everyone likes to do it, it's easy, but for a little extra time I don't know why it's any more effort to light up some hardwood charcoal. It really adds flavor to your food."

One of Kerry's favorite tailgate dishes is his Smoky Venison Chili. The recipe isn't hard, but there's a long list of ingredients. Kerry suggests making it a day or two ahead and reheating it in the parking lot.

Smoky Venison Chili

Mix the spices and store in an airtight container until ready to use. Chop celery, onion, garlic, and bell pepper and set aside in a large bowl. Chop potato and set aside in another bowl.

Fry chopped bacon in a 13-inch skillet or 3- to 5-quart Dutch oven over medium-high heat until crisp. Remove bacon with slotted spoon and set aside in a large bowl. Brown chopped ham in bacon fat. Remove with slotted spoon, and set aside with bacon. Brown ground venison in bacon fat, breaking it up while it cooks. Remove with slotted spoon and set aside with ham and bacon. Venison will soak up most of the bacon fat, so add some vegetable oil to the skillet, and fry potatoes until lightly browned. Remove potatoes and add to bowl with meat.

Add vegetables to the skillet (with a little more oil) and sauté until lightly browned (about 10 minutes). Add beer and beef broth to the vegetables, and return all meat and potatoes to the skillet. Add jalapenos and/or optional habaneros. Mix very, very well while slowly adding all the spice mixture until it's well incorporated. Mixture should turn an attractive reddish-brown color. Cover and simmer on low heat 20 to 30 minutes, stirring occasionally (if mixture starts to look too dry, add a bit more beer or beef broth).

Then add canned tomatoes with juice, dark red beans with juice, and chipotle peppers with adobo sauce. Mix well.

Simmer for another 15 to 20 more minutes, stirring occasionally. Add optional ingredients, such as Frank's Red Hot or Worcestershire sauce, if desired.

Serves 8 to 12.

INGREDIENTS:

½ pound good, smoky bacon, chopped into ¼-inch–½-inch chunks

½ pound good, smoke-cured ham, cut into ½-inch–1-inch chunks

2 pounds ground venison

5 stalks celery, chopped

2 large onions, chopped

8 cloves garlic, chopped

1 green bell pepper, chopped

2 potatoes, chopped

8 to 12 ounces Schlenkerla Rauchbier (Bavarian smoked beer), or substitute with dark porter or stout

1 cup beef broth

6 fresh jalapenos, roughly chopped (leave in the seeds for hotter chili)

Optional: 2 fresh habanero peppers, finely chopped (for very hot chili)

1 14.5-ounce can of tomatoes, chopped or diced

1 15.5-ounce can of dark red kidney beans (they must be "dark red" beans or they'll lose their color)

1 7-ounce can of chipotle peppers in adobo sauce

2 to 4 tablespoons vegetable oil or olive oil

Optional: Frank's Red Hot, to taste

Optional: Worcestershire sauce, to taste

FOR THE SPICE MIXTURE:

3 tablespoons cumin

1 tablespoon kosher salt

1 tablespoon smoked paprika (or substitute with regular paprika)

1 tablespoon cayenne pepper

1 tablespoon chili powder

1 teaspoon cinnamon

1 teaspoon oregano

1 teaspoon coarsely ground black pepper, or to taste

8 to 12 juniper berries, crushed

Maple Pork Chops

Preheat the grill to medium-high heat.

Season the pork chops with salt and pepper to taste. Grill the pork until desired doneness.

In a saucepan combine the rest of the ingredients and cook over high heat until mixture becomes syrupy, 5–7 minutes, stirring frequently. Drizzle sauce over pork and serve.

Serves 4.

INGREDIENTS:

4 boneless pork loin chops

Salt and pepper

1 tablespoon olive oil

1 tablespoon balsamic vinegar

¼ cup maple syrup

¼ cup chicken broth

2 teaspoons Dijon mustard

Easy Mediterranean Chicken

Combine first 5 ingredients in a bowl and set aside.

Preheat grill to medium-high.

Season chicken with salt and pepper to taste and place on the grill. Cook until done. Serve topped with salsa.

Serves 4.

INGREDIENTS:

¾ cup chunky-style salsa (bottled is fine)

⅓ cup plum tomato, chopped

⅓ cup zucchini, chopped

¼ cup black olives, chopped

2 teaspoons capers

4 Boneless chicken breasts

Salt

Pepper

Photo: T.J. Hamilton

Grilled Bourbon Salmon

Combine all ingredients except salmon. Pour into a zip-top bag and add the salmon. Marinate in the refrigerator for 2 hours. Turn the bag occasionally to coat evenly.

Preheat the grill to high.

Remove the salmon from the marinade and place on the grill. Cook until fish flakes easily, about 6 minutes.

Serves 4.

INGREDIENTS:

- ¼ cup bourbon
- ¼ cup orange juice
- ¼ cup low-sodium soy sauce
- ¼ cup brown sugar, packed
- ¼ cup green onions, chopped
- 3 tablespoons fresh chives, chopped
- 2 garlic cloves, chopped
- 4 salmon fillets

Photo: David Snodgress

Grill-top Potatoes

Tear a large piece of aluminum foil (or use two sheets) to form a "boat" large enough to hold ingredients and wrap them loosely. Combine all ingredients into the foil boat and wrap the foil loosely around them and seal.

Preheat the grill to low–medium heat.

Place foil boat on the grill and cook for 45 minutes to 1 hour, shaking occasionally to mix ingredients.

Serves 4–6.

INGREDIENTS:

- 2 large potatoes, cut into 1-inch cubes
- 1 ½ pounds smoked or summer sausage, cut into 1-inch pieces
- 1 cup small mushrooms
- 1 large white onion, chopped
- 1 bell pepper, sliced thin from top to bottom
- 2 celery stalks, cut into ½-inch pieces
- Several dashes hot sauce
- ¼ stick of butter, sliced thin
- Salt and pepper (to taste)
- Several dashes Worcestershire

SEAN SQUIRES'S GRILLED OYSTERS & "BUC'S BREW

Sean Squires is the executive chef at the Island Way Grill and Salt Rock Grill, eateries he co-owns with Tampa Bay Buccaneers Mike Alstott and Dave Moore.

While Mike and Dave are inside putting on pads and prepping for the game, Sean is in the parking lot putting food on the grill and preparing his Buc's Brew. He is a chef, so he likes to play with flavors and new dishes on game day. So when Tampa was named one of America's top grilling cities in the country he created a new dish to celebrate, Cheddar Parmesan Ranch Grilled Oysters.

"One of the reasons I picked oysters," Sean explains, "was because oysters are indigenous to our Gulf Coast here. I made a simple recipe . . . but it is delicate. You don't want to grill it too long because it is going to continue to cook when you have it shell side down throughout the shell. When that shell heats up, it will cook pretty fast."

Cheddar Parmesan Ranch Grilled Oysters

Light grill using Kingsford® Charcoal with Sure Fire Grooves.™

Mix breadcrumbs, olive oil, lemon juice, Ranch mix, fennel tops and bulbs, and bacon in a bowl; set aside.

Drizzle each oyster with Cheddar Parmesan Ranch dressing. Grill oysters, shell side down, for about 1 ½ minutes.

Top each oyster with about a teaspoon of remaining Parmesan Cheddar Ranch dressing, then pack with bread-

INGREDIENTS:

- 12 fresh gulf oysters, on the half shell*
- 6 tablespoons Hidden Valley® Cheddar Parmesan Ranch dressing
- 1 cup Panko breadcrumbs
- ½ cup olive oil
- 2 tablespoons freshly squeezed lemon juice
- 1 packet Hidden Valley® Original Ranch® Salad Dressing & Seasoning Mix
- 2 tablespoons fennel tops, minced
- 1 ½ tablespoons fennel bulbs, finely diced
- 4 slices bacon, cooked and diced
- ½ cup finely grated Cheddar cheese

crumb mixture. Sprinkle each oyster with cheese and place back on grill. Cover with lid or pan; grill until cheese melts and breadcrumb mixture is crisp.

*Ask the seafood department at your local grocer to shuck the oysters on the half shell.

Serves 2.

Sean's "High Octane Buc's Brew"

In addition to his food, Sean is known around the parking lot for his Buc's Brew, which he says goes with just about everything.

Combine all ingredients and mix vigorously until well blended. Pour over ice.

Note: This recipe is for two servings; mix the drink in glasses. If you want to make a larger batch, use the same ingredients and make it as strong or weak as you like, preparing it in a large cooler with very little ice. Then add ice to each person's cup and pour the Brew over the ice.

INGREDIENTS:

2 ounces cognac

2 ounces Grey Goose

2 ounces Pama (Pomegranate Liquor) or pomegranate juice

2 ounces Sour Mix

2 ounces orange juice

6 ounces Rock Star (or other energy drink)

Cilantro Corn

Preheat grill to medium-high.

Tear-off eight sheets of aluminum foil and place one slice of butter about 2 inches from the end of each sheet. Place one ear of corn on top of each butter slice, season with salt, and sprinkle cilantro on top. Roll up the foil around the corn and seal the ends.

Place corn on the grill and cook, turning 2–3 times, until done, about 10–15 minutes.

Serves 8.

INGREDIENTS:

4 tablespoons butter, cut into 8 slices

8 ears corn, shucked

Salt

1 bunch cilantro, chopped

Herb Lamb Chops

Place the first five ingredients in a food processor and pulse until mixed. Pour in olive oil and pulse into a paste. Rub the paste on both sides of the lamb chops being sure to cover all surface areas. Place in a zip-top bag and marinate in the refrigerator for at least 2 hours.

Preheat the grill to high.

Grill the lamb chops for 2–3 minutes. Then flip and cook on the other side for 2–3 minutes more until done.

Serves 3–6.

INGREDIENTS:

1 tablespoon fresh rosemary leaves

1 teaspoon fresh thyme leaves

2 large garlic cloves, crushed

⅛ teaspoon cayenne pepper

Kosher salt

2 tablespoons olive oil

6 lamb chops

Photo: Ed Rode

Photo: Scott Eklund

Lemon Asparagus

Remove tough ends of asparagus and remove scales. Melt butter in a skillet, add asparagus, and sauté until tender (about 3 minutes). Add salt and pepper. Remove from heat and add lemon rind and lemon juice. Toss the asparagus in the mixture and then serve.

Serves 4–6.

INGREDIENTS:

- 2 pounds fresh asparagus
- ¼ cup butter
- ½ teaspoon salt
- ½ teaspoon pepper
- 1 tablespoon lemon rind
- ¼ cup fresh lemon juice

Orange Leg of Lamb

In a bowl, combine the thyme, garlic, orange peel, salt, and pepper. Mix well. Trim any excess fat from the lamb and lay it, opened, on a cutting board; cut about a dozen slits in each side about ½" deep. Fill each slit with some of the spice mixture and rub the remaining mixture all over both sides of the meat. Brush the olive oil on both sides of the meat and let sit at room temperature for 1 ½ – 2 hours. (You can make this a day ahead and refrigerate it, but be sure it rests at room temperature before grilling.)

Preheat grill to medium-high.

Place lamb on the grill and cook for 7-9 minutes per side (for medium rare) or until meat reaches preferred doneness. Remove from the grill and let rest 10 – 15 minutes before slicing and serving.

Serves 8–10.

INGREDIENTS:

- 1 ½ tablespoons fresh thyme, chopped
- 3 cloves garlic, minced
- 1 ½ tablespoons grated orange peel
- 1 ½ teaspoon kosher salt
- 1 ½ teaspoon black pepper
- 1 Boneless leg of lamb (about 4 pounds)
- Olive oil

PATRICK MOULD'S CRAWFISH ETOUFFEE

Some of the best tailgate menus you'll ever taste are in Louisiana. A day at an LSU tailgate party can be a culinary treat.

Louisianan Patrick Mould knows a lot about the Cajun and Creole cuisines. He's a chef, a television personality, and a tailgater. "I think it's one of the defining regional cuisines in America," he says.

"There're really two separate styles of cuisines in Louisiana, Cajun and Creole. Cajun is a very rustic style of cuisine. It's hardy one pot dishes . . . their style of cooking is less sophisticated than their Creole cousins. The Creole style of cooking is based in New Orleans, and Creole is a term associated with anyone whose parents were not born in Louisiana but they were, and that includes French, Spanish, Italian, Africans, and Native Americans who were at some point mixed up down there in New Orleans. And their style of cooking is much more sophisticated. It's based on the European style of cooking, a lot of sauces and pan sautéed filets of fish and not as rustic as Cajun style, but they're using all the same ingredients."

One of the best-known Cajun dishes is, of course, Etouffee. Patrick's is a good one.

Pat's Crawfish Etouffee

In a saucepot, heat butter over medium heat. Cook onions and garlic for 5 minutes. Add flour and thyme; cook for 1 minute, being careful not to brown flour.

Add chicken broth, Creole seasoning, paprika, and hot sauce. Cook for an additional 2 minutes. Stir in crawfish, cover, lower heat, and simmer for 10 minutes, stirring occasionally. Stir in green onions and parsley. Serve with cooked Toro Brand Rice.

Serves 4.

© Chef Patrick Mould, Louisiana Culinary Enterprises, Inc.

INGREDIENTS:

1 stick unsalted butter
3 cups minced onions
1 tablespoon minced garlic
4 teaspoons flour
1 ½ teaspoons dried thyme leaves
1 cup chicken broth
1 tablespoon Tony Chachere's Creole Seasoning
1 teaspoon paprika
1 teaspoon hot sauce
1 pound crawfish tails
¼ cup chopped green onions
2 tablespoons chopped parsley
4 cups cooked Toro Brand Rice

STEVE RAICHLEN'S SWEET & SMOKY RIBS

Steven Raichlen is an author, television host, and grilling authority, as well as the professor at Barbecue University . . . which is both a barbecue cooking program and a television show. Yeah, this guy knows his way around a grill. And he knows the mistake most tailgate chefs make: "Specifically in terms of the grill, overcrowding the grill."

"If you watch me grill on the TV show you'll see I never have more than half the grate filled with food. I always leave myself plenty of space so if I get a flare up or something starts to cook too quickly I can always move it to a cooler section of the grill."

His other tip for tailgaters is to spend some time preparing before the game and don't hold back. "Remember that there should be an element of the theatre of dramatics at a tailgate picnic," Steven says. "You're not just trying to feed them you're trying to 'wow' them."

St. Louis, Mo. Super Smokers Sweet and Smoky Dry Rub Ribs

Remove the thin, papery membrane from the back of each rack of ribs: Turn a rack meat side down. Insert a sharp implement, such as the tip of a meat thermometer, under the membrane (the best place to start is right next to the first rib bone). Using a dishcloth or pliers to gain a secure grip, pull off the membrane. Repeat with the remaining racks.

Place the ribs on baking sheets.

Place the brown sugar, salt, and pepper in a bowl and stir to mix well. (Actually your fingers work better for mixing a rub than a spoon or whisk does.) Sprinkle this rub all over the ribs on both sides, patting it onto the meat with your fingertips. Cover the ribs with plastic wrap and let cure in the refrigerator for 3 hours.

INGREDIENTS:

4 racks baby back pork ribs (6 to 8 pounds total)

2 cups firmly packed brown sugar

½ cup coarse salt (kosher or sea)

¼ cup freshly ground black pepper

Dr Pepper barbecue sauce, for serving (below)

YOU'LL ALSO NEED:

2 cups wood chips or chunks (preferably apple), soaked for 1 hour in water to cover, then drained

rib rack

Set up the grill for indirect grilling and preheat to medium.

If using a gas grill, place all of the wood chips or chunks in the smoker box or smoker pouch and run the grill on high until you see smoke, then reduce the heat to medium. If using a charcoal grill, place a large drip pan in the center, preheat the grill to medium, then toss all of the wood chips or chunks on the coals.

When ready to cook, using damp paper towels, wipe the excess rub off the ribs. Place the ribs, preferably on a rib rack, in the center of the hot grate, over the drip pan and away from the heat. Cover the grill and cook the ribs until tender, 1 ¼ to 1 ½ hours.

When the ribs are done, they'll be handsomely browned and the meat will have shrunk back about ¼ inch from the ends of the bones. Transfer the cooked ribs to a platter or cutting board. Serve them as whole racks, cut the racks into pieces, or carve them into individual ribs. Serve them with the St. Louis-style barbecue sauce.

Yield: Serves 4 really hungry people or 8 folks with average appetites.

Dr. Pepper Barbecue Sauce

Cut the lemon in half cross wise and cut a ¼-inch slice off of one half. Remove any seeds in this slice. Juice the remaining lemon: you should have 2 to 3 tablespoons juice.

Place the lemon slice, 2 tablespoons of the lemon juice, and the garlic, onion slice, Dr Pepper, ketchup, Worcestershire sauce, steak sauce, hot sauce, vinegar, liquid smoke, and pepper in a heavy nonreactive saucepan and gradually bring to a boil over medium heat.

Reduce the heat slightly to maintain a gentle simmer. Let the sauce simmer gently until thick and richly flavored, 10 to 15 minutes. Taste for seasoning, adding more lemon

INGREDIENTS:

- 1 large juicy lemon
- 1 clove garlic, peeled and lightly crushed with the side of a cleaver
- 1 thin (¼-inch) slice onion
- 1 cup Dr Pepper
- ¾ cup ketchup
- 3 tablespoons Worcestershire sauce
- 2 tablespoons A.1. steak sauce
- 1 tablespoon of your favorite hot sauce, or more to taste
- 1 tablespoon cider vinegar, or more to taste
- 1 teaspoon liquid smoke
- ½ teaspoon freshly ground black pepper
- Coarse salt (kosher or sea)

juice, hot sauce, and/or vinegar as necessary and seasoning with salt to taste, if desired.

Strain the sauce into a bowl (or clean glass jars) and let cool to room temperature, then refrigerate, covered, until serving. The sauce will keep for several months in the refrigerator.

Bring to room temperature before serving.

Yield: Makes about 2 cups

Recipe from Barbecue USA by Steven Raichlen (Workman).

Photo: Ed Rode

TOMMY THOMPSON'S GRILLED PORK LOIN

During the week he's Tommy Thompson. On Sunday he's Finchef, host of the Fintinki tailgate party outside Dolphin Stadium in Miami. But this is no ordinary tailgate party. Tommy—who is also a real, live professional chef—has complete, planned menus for every game that would be as appropriate for a white tablecloth restaurant as the asphalt.

"You can go a step above. Have the ordinary but go extraordinary above that. It makes a difference; people notice this. It's rewarding, it really is. It makes for a nice experience when people see something above the bratwurst, above the hamburger. There's nothing wrong with that, but it's nice to have a whole tenderloin on the grill."

That can be intimidating. Tommy sees that in tailgaters around him, too. But his counsel is not to worry about that; expand your menu and have some fun. "Fear of failure in front of your friends . . . you can't have that. I mean, the people around you are your friends."

Grill-top Pork Loin with Cinnamon-Cane Syrup Brush

Rub pork loin with, in order, mustard, garlic, ginger, and half of cinnamon. Roast in 325˚ F oven for about 40 minutes. (Note: Pork is still fairly pink inside.) Let rest overnight in fridge. Mix remainder of cinnamon and cane syrup and use for basting liquid on grill top next day. Slice and serve.

INGREDIENTS:

1 whole 10–12 pound center cut pork loin

8 tablespoons cinnamon

6 tablespoons chopped garlic

4 tablespoons chopped ginger

1 12-ounce jar of Creole or whole grain mustard

1 quart of unfiltered cane syrup. (Most grocery stores have this item.)

2 cups kosher salt

Cracked black pepper corns

DIM COOKERS

If you're looking for great barbecue a good place to start is Texas. And if you're in Houston you'll find it coming off the grill of the Dimozine (see page 53 for more on this tricked-out tailgate rig). The Dimozine is the trailer/smoker of a group of guys who call themselves DIM Cookers. In addition to competing in barbecue contests in the Lone Star State, these guys are big Texans tailgaters. They'll feed more than 100 people before kickoff and have more food waiting for you after the game.

Their ribs, brisket, and other dishes are award winners, and they say the secret ingredient is time. "One thing about barbecuing is you have to take your time," say DIM Cookers' Tad Cook and John Swazey. "We cook brisket for about 12 hours, the ribs take about 6, chicken takes about 4, and you just can't be in a hurry or you'll mess it up."

Of course your seasonings make a big difference, too. "We basically use a salt, paprika, black pepper sort of rub. We rub the meat down real good. A lot of time we'll use a marinade and use these big syringes and inject all the meat to get the marinade down inside the brisket and let them sit in the ice box overnight to soak up the ingredients. Then we put them on the pits the next morning."

DIM's Pork Ribs

Preheat smoker to 225°–250° F. In a bowl combine generous amounts, to taste, of the salt, pepper, and paprika to create a rub. Work the rub into the meat thoroughly. Place the meat in the smoker, bone side up. Be sure to avoid having the meat in direct flames, using a shield if necessary. Cook for 2 to 3 hours or until the meat pulls back ½ to ¾ inch from the bone tips.

INGREDIENTS:
- Lawry's Season Salt
- Freshly ground black pepper
- Paprika
- 3 racks of pork ribs, with knuckles on
- Barbecue sauce

Remove the meat from the smoker and place it on aluminum foil (with the edges folded up to create a "boat") and apply your favorite barbecue sauce—but avoid really sweet sauces since they tend to gum up when cooked for a long period. Wrap the foil "boat" shut to seal in the sauce and place it in the cooker for 1 hour more.

Note: If you're cooking with a gas grill, buy some Liquid Smoke and pour it on several times during cooking to get the flavor a charcoal or wood fire would naturally give the meat.

Makes 10 to 15 servings.

MARK PRECE'S FIRECRACKER PASTA SALAD

Mark Prece knows his pasta. As Corporate Executive Chef for Mueller's, Heartland and Golden Grain pasta, he works with it every day. So it should be no surprise that he's an evangelist for adding pasta to your tailgate menu, and he says it isn't as much of a stretch as you may first think.

"People love pasta," he explains. "Pasta is a great food, kind of a stick-to-your-ribs food for the tailgating season. It's what we call a comfort food. Usually if there's pasta on the table with all the other ingredients it's one of the ones people really like to try and taste."

The easiest way to integrate pasta into your menu is, of course, as a salad. You can prepare it ahead, and it's ready to serve as soon as you're set up in the parking lot. But Mark says don't be afraid to use warm pasta dishes, too; just wrap them up and put them in a cooler and take them to the game (coolers keep hot things warm, too).

His Rotini Firecracker Pasta Salad isn't one of those hot dishes, but it is a great way to utilize leftover BBQ or deli meats.

Rotini Firecracker Pasta Salad

Cook pastas according to package directions. When pasta is al dente, drain in colander. Rinse pasta with cold water until cool to the touch. Drain well. Put pasta in large mixing bowl and add onions, pepper, and meat, and toss well. Next mix in all remaining ingredients and blend well. Chill, sprinkle with scallions, and serve.

INGREDIENTS:

- 1 pound rotini (you can substitute whole-grain pasta for regular semolina if you prefer)
- 1 cup yellow onion, diced
- 1 cup green bell peppers, diced
- 1 cup red bell peppers, diced
- 12 ounce BBQ ham, beef, or chicken, diced
- 2 ½ cups ranch dressing
- ⅓ cups BBQ sauce
- ⅓ cups Parmesan cheese
- ¼ cups grated scallions, minced
- Salt and Pepper to taste

Texas Chili

In a large skillet brown the beef in the vegetable oil. Drain off most of the fat and add the onions, garlic, and green pepper to the skillet. Sauté for 5 minutes until soft, stirring constantly. Add the next 6 ingredients. (If you prefer your chili thicker mix the flour and 2 tablespoons of water in a small bowl and stir the mixture into the chili.) Turn down the heat and simmer for 30 minutes. Add the beans, stir, and let simmer another 10 minutes. Serve in a bowl topped with the cheese of your choice.

Tip: This is a great dish to prepare a day or two before the game, refrigerate, and then warm up on the grill before serving at your tailgate party.

Serves 6–8.

INGREDIENTS:

- 2 pounds ground beef
- 1 ¼ cups vegetable oil
- 1 cup onion, chopped
- 2 garlic cloves, minced
- 1 large green pepper, cut into strips
- 3 tablespoons chili powder
- 2 teaspoons sugar
- 3 ½ cups canned whole tomatoes
- 1 cup tomato sauce
- 1 cup water
- ½ teaspoon salt (or to taste)
- 1 tablespoon all purpose flour (optional)
- 2 tablespoons water (optional)
- 2 cups kidney beans
- Mozzarella or cheddar cheese, shredded (for topping)

Jalapeno Steak

Combine the first 7 ingredients in a blender and puree. Pour the mixture on both sides of the steak and rub all over. Place in a zip-top bag or covered glass dish and marinate for one day in the refrigerator.

Preheat grill to medium.

Grill marinated steak to preferred doneness, turning once. Cut steak into slices and serve.

Serves 6–8.

INGREDIENTS:

- 3–4 jalapeno peppers
- 1 tablespoon salt
- ¼ cup lime juice
- ½ cup olive oil
- 4 garlic cloves
- ½ tablespoon ground black pepper
- 1 tablespoon dried oregano
- 1 2-pound steak

LISA TALAMINI'S MARGARITA PORK KEBABS

Lisa Talamini is all about tailgating light. But she's not about losing taste while you're losing weight.

Every time you pick up a newspaper it seems to have a story about obesity in America. As a country we're overweight, and as the chief nutritionist and program director for Jenny Craig, Lisa is well aware of the struggles we have eating right. That can be even harder at a tailgate party where the typical menu isn't exactly fat-free.

Harder, but doable.

"It's really about just making some small changes that over time, if you tailgate on a regular basis, can really give you some great, big results," Lisa explains. "And that's about looking at the ingredients and skinnying up some of the ingredients, and skinnying up the cuts of meat you choose, and skinnying up the prep. There're some great ways you can still enjoy the foods you love in moderation.

"Ribs are a great example because there are a lot of types of ribs you can buy. If you look at back ribs they're very high in fat; they're about 34 grams of fat for a 4-ounce portion. If you look at country-style ribs they go to 24 grams of fat for a 4-ounce portion. So just by even making that change you can save yourself some fat."

If you want to cut down on the fat even more, Lisa says to look for alternatives—like swapping the ribs for pork tenderloin, which has 7 grams of fat in that 4-ounce portion. Lisa also suggests swapping other ingredients—such as sauces for rubs and chips for carrots—to cut down on calories and fat without losing flavor.

Margarita Pork Kebabs

Combine margarita mix, coriander, and garlic. Place pork cubes in heavy plastic bag; pour marinade over to cover. Marinate for at least 30 minutes.

Blend together well the butter, lime juice, sugar, and parsley; set aside.

Thread port cubes onto skewers, alternating with pieces of corn and pepper. (If using bamboo skewers, soak in water 20–30 minutes before using.) Grill over hot coals, basting with butter mixture, for 15–20 minutes, turning frequently.

INGREDIENTS:

- 1 cup margarita drink mix (OR: 1 cup lime juice, 4 teaspoons sugar, ½ teaspoon salt)
- 1 teaspoon ground coriander
- 1 clove garlic, minced
- 1 pound pork tenderloin, cut into 1-inch cubes
- 2 tablespoons butter, softened
- 2 teaspoons lime juice
- ⅛ teaspoon sugar
- 1 tablespoon minced parsley
- 2 ears corn, cut into 8 pieces
- 1 large green or red pepper, cut into 1-inch cubes

Recipe courtesy of Jenny Craig *Taste of the Grill* and the National Pork Board.

Mahi Mahi

In a bowl combine the cilantro, pineapple juice, 2 table-spoons olive oil, honey, garlic, and cayenne pepper and mix well. Pour marinade into a zip-top bag and add the fillets.

Marinate in the refrigerator or cooler for 2 hours, up to overnight.

Preheat grill to high heat.

Place fish on grill and top with a pad of butter. Cook for 5–6 minutes until done.

Meanwhile, brush the pineapple slices on both sides with remaining olive oil and season with salt and pepper to taste. Place on another section of the grill and cook for 1–2 minutes on each side.

When fish and pineapple slices are done, remove from the grill and serve one filet topped with a grilled pineapple slice.

Serves 6.

INGREDIENTS:
- 6 mahi mahi fillets
- ¼ cup chopped cilantro
- ¼ cup pineapple juice
- 2 ½ tablespoons olive oil, divided
- 1 tablespoon honey
- 3 cloves garlic, minced
- 1 teaspoon cayenne pepper
- 1 can pineapple slices
- ½ stick of butter
- Salt and pepper to taste

Photo: Jon Bower

Photo: Mike Yoder

Barbecue Chicken Pizza

Preheat grill to medium–high.

Salt and pepper the chicken breast and grill until internal temperature is 150°F. Remove from the grill, let cool, and cut into ½-inch think slices.

Place the crust on a 14-inch pizza pan. Spread the barbecue sauce evenly over the crust, and top it with the onions and chicken. In a bowl mix the cheeses, and sprinkle them evenly on the pizza. Place the pizza on the grill and cook for 10 to 15 minutes, until the crust is crisp and the cheese has melted.

Makes 4 to 8 servings.

INGREDIENTS:

2 skinless, boneless chicken breasts

Salt and pepper

1 (14-inch) pizza crust (store-bought dough is fine)

¾ cup barbecue sauce

½ red onion, thinly sliced

6 ounces Mozzarella cheese, shredded

3 ounces Parmesan cheese, shredded

Feta and Tomato Pizza

Preheat grill to medium.

Brush tomatoes with oil and grill for 1–2 minutes without turning them. Remove and set aside.

Place the crust on a 14-inch pizza pan. Brush the crust with oil and place the tomatoes on top. Meanwhile, mix the remaining ingredients in a bowl and sprinkle on top of the pizza. Place the pizza on the grill, and cook until the cheese is melted and bubbling slightly.

Serves 4–8.

INGREDIENTS:

Olive oil

6 tomatoes, cut into slices

1 14-inch pizza crust (store-bought is fine)

1 cup feta cheese

½ cup fresh basil, chopped

1 teaspoon salt

½ teaspoon black pepper

MIKE ZELLER'S QUESO DE SALSA SAUSAGE SOUP

Mike Zeller has what for many tailgaters is a dream job.

He's a chef, but not just any chef. Mike is the top chef at Johnsonville, the company whose brats are on grills at every stadium in the country every weekend. In places like Green Bay, Chicago, and Pittsburgh you'll find tailgaters cooking them so many different ways, you'll lose count. But perhaps the most popular way is on the grill and in a beer bath.

Which leads to an argument you hear across America: What beer is best with those brats? Well, let's let the guy who creates these flavors tell us.

"What I always tell people to do is the beer you enjoy drinking is the beer you want to use in that beer bath. If you like a dark beer and you like that more hops and barley flavor, then use a dark beer. If you don't, and you like a lighter beer, then look for a lighter beer."

Simple enough. Which is also how cooking brats can be. The key to it is temperature and time. You should heat your grill to 250°–300°F, and you should take your time.

"You don't want to grill bratwurst like you grill chicken or steak or something like that," explains Mike. "When you're grilling sausage you want to do that slow-and-low. You want to turn them every 3–4 minutes; it will take you about 20–25 minutes."

But brats are more versatile than just something to grill. They can be part of the recipe, not the recipe itself. Mike urges cooks to have fun and experiment, which is how he comes up with dishes as diverse as Creole Fettuccine and Queso de Salsa Sausage Soup.

Queso de Salsa Sausage Soup

Grill brats according to directions. Cool slightly and slice into ¼-inch coin slices, reserve for later. In a medium-size pot add cheese sauce, beer, salsa, corn, and cilantro and place on the hottest part of the grill. Make sure to use a pot that has handles that will not burn or melt. Blend well.

Bring mixture to a simmer and add sliced bratwurst. Simmer for 5 minutes, stirring often.

INGREDIENTS:

- 1 package Johnsonville fresh brats, grill according to package
- 1 16-ounce jar double cheddar cheese sauce (Ragu)
- 1 12-ounce bottle beer, light or dark
- 1 16-ounce jar cilantro salsa (Pace)
- 2 cups frozen whole kernel corn
- 1 tablespoon chopped fresh cilantro

Options: Replace bratwurst with chorizo or any other spicy type of Johnsonville sausage.

Photo: Jerry Lai

Dark Beer Brats

Preheat grill to medium-high.

Place an aluminum foil baking pan on the grill and add the first three ingredients. Just as the mixture begins to boil reduce the heat to low to simmer.

Meanwhile, grill the bratwurst over low-medium heat until cooked through. Transfer brats into beer mixture and let simmer for 15–20 minutes before serving. The mixture can also be used as a holding tray for the brats to keep them warm for any stragglers.

Serves 5.

INGREDIENTS:

- 4 cans dark beer (brown ales, bocks, and porters are good choices)
- ½ stick butter
- 1 large onion, sliced
- 1 package bratwurst

Chicken Kebabs

Alternately thread the chicken, peppers, and onions on metal skewers and place in a shallow backing dish. Set aside.

Combine the remaining ingredients in a bowl and mix well. Pour mixture over the skewers, being sure to evenly coat the chicken. Cover and refrigerate for 1–2 hours.

Preheat grill to medium–high.

Place the skewers on the grill and cook for 4–5 minutes. Turn and cook an additional 4–5 minutes until done.

Serves 6–8.

INGREDIENTS:

- 1 ½ pounds skinless, boneless chicken breasts, cut into 1½-inch pieces
- 4 bell peppers, quartered
- 4 onions, cut into 1-inch chunks
- ½ cup soy sauce
- 2 tablespoons sugar
- 1 teaspoon olive oil
- 1 clove garlic, minced

Photo: Ed Rode

Steak Fajitas

Season the meat with salt and pepper to taste. Place seasoned steak in a large zip-top bag and add the picante sauce. Flip the bag a few times to coat the meat and place in the refrigerator to marinate for at least 4 hours up to overnight.

Preheat grill to high heat.

Place steak on grill and cook for 7 minutes on both sides or to desired doneness. Remove from the grill and let rest for 5–10 minutes before slicing.

Meanwhile place olive oil in a hot pan and sauté peppers and onions. Place the sliced steak in a tortilla and top with pepper, onions, cheese, and guacamole and sour cream, if desired.

Serves 6–8

INGREDIENTS:

3 pounds skirt steak

2 tablespoons kosher salt

4 tablespoons pepper

1 24-ounce jar picante sauce–hot

1 ½ tablespoons olive oil

2 red bell peppers, cut into strips

2 green bell peppers, cut into strips

1 large onion, cut into strips

1 cup cheddar cheese, grated

Guacamole and sour cream (if desired)

Flour tortillas

Easy Chili

Brown beef in oil. Add garlic and cook 2 minutes. Add chili powder, flour, oregano, cumin, and paprika. Cook until meat is well coated. Add 2 cans broth and stir.

Partially cover and simmer 45 minutes, stirring occasionally. Add 1 can of broth if you prefer a soupier consistency. Season with salt and pepper to taste. Add beans. Partially cover and simmer 45 minutes–1 hour more.

Remove pan from heat; cool and refrigerate overnight.

At your tailgate reheat the chili and serve garnished with cheese.

Serves 6–8

INGREDIENTS:

3 pounds chuck roast, cut into 1-inch pieces

Olive oil

2 cloves garlic, minced

6 tablespoons ancho chili powder

5 tablespoons flour

1 tablespoon dried oregano

1 teaspoon cumin

1 tablespoon sweet paprika

2–3 cans beef broth

Salt

Pepper

1 can drained pinto beans (use 2 cans if desired)

Cheddar cheese for garnish (optional)

MIKE MILLS'S APPLE CITY RIBS

Around a race track you just have to say "The King" and everyone knows who you're talking about. Around a barbecue pit you just have to say "The Legend" and everyone knows you're talking about Mike Mills.

Mike is the only three-time Memphis in May World Grand Champion, he's won more than 100 barbecue competitions over-all, he owns six barbecue restaurants, and he's written an award-winning barbecue cookbook. So when he offers tips to tailgaters about how to barbecue, you'd be wise to listen.

One of the biggest challenges for tailgaters who want to cook true, low-and-slow barbecue is that it takes several hours, and you may not be in the parking lot long enough to pull if off. After all, some recipes leave the meat on the grill or in the smoker for 6, 8, 10 hours or more. Many stadiums will let you arrive just 4 hours before kickoff. What's a tailgater to do?

"Well, you can pre-start some things at home and do the marinating, which will help speed up the cooking process," answers Mike. But his main tip for cutting down cooking time is cutting down the meat. "You can still do some brisket and cook it in 2 or 3 hours if you do some marinating, but you don't use a 10-pound piece of meat that you're trying to cook on a small grill. You cut it down in size and maybe you have 2-pound pieces of meat instead.

"You can cover more surface area on your grill and still leave some space for your heated area and have more indirect heat."

His other tip for great barbecue is don't mess with the meat and keep turning it over. "Moving it around is different than turning it over," he says. "You can pick up a piece of meat and move it to a cooler spot if it's getting too hot or cooking faster that the others. Moving it around on the grill does not hurt it. Flipping it over to drive the juices in and out and breaking the meat apart is what actually dries it out."

And Mike says don't ever use a fork to check the meat or move it. That's a sure way to have the juices pour out, and if you do it often enough you'll drain it dry.

Apple City Barbecue Grand World Champion Ribs

INGREDIENTS:

4 racks of ribs (about 2 pounds each)

Magic Dust (see recipe below)

4 cups apple juice in a spray bottle

Apple City Barbecue Sauce (see recipe below)

Sprinkle the ribs liberally with Magic Dust, coating both sides. Put them in a shallow pan or on a cookie sheet and cover them with clear plastic wrap or a lid. Refrigerate them until you're ready to use them. I recommend letting them marinate for at least an hour. At the restaurant, we dust the ribs up to a day in advance.

Preheat the grill or smoker.

Soak the apple wood chips in water for half an hour. Drain.

Remove the grate and arrange the medium-hot coals in a grill or smoker. If you are using a grill, it must have a lid. Set an aluminum pan next to the coals as a drip pan. Spread out the wet wood chips on the coals. Replace the rack, close the grill, and check the temperature. It should be between 200°–210° F degrees. If the temperature is too high, open the lid to allow some heat to escape.

Once the temperature is steady, place the ribs on the rack, bone side down. You want to cook them bone side down as much as possible. If necessary, you can cut the racks of ribs in half to comfortably fit your grill.

Cover and smoke the ribs for about 1 ½ hours or until the ribs are done and tender.

You'll want to check the ribs every 20 minutes or so. Examine them to see if the surface of the meat looks dry or moist. Ribs "sweat" about three times during the smoking process. When they're sweating, mop or mist them with some apple juice and sprinkle them with a little more Magic Dust. Opening the lid will lower the temperature; add more coals and wood chips as needed to maintain the temperature.

About 10 minutes before you remove the ribs from the pit, mop them with the sauce. When you take them off the pit, mop again with sauce and sprinkle some more Magic Dust on them. Serve immediately.

Serves 4, or you can cut the racks in half to serve 8.

Magic Dust

Mix all ingredients and store in a tightly covered container. To make it a little more hot and spicy, increase the mustard powder and black pepper to ¼ cup each.

Makes about 2 ½ cups.

INGREDIENTS:

- ½ cup paprika
- ¼ cup kosher salt, finely ground
- ¼ cup sugar
- 2 tablespoons mustard powder
- ¼ cup chili powder
- ¼ cup ground cumin
- 2 tablespoons ground black pepper
- ¼ cup granulated garlic
- 2 tablespoons cayenne

Apple City Barbecue Sauce

Combine the ketchup, rice vinegar, apple juice or cider, cider vinegar, brown sugar, soy sauce or Worcestershire sauce, mustard, garlic powder, white pepper, cayenne, and bacon bits in a large saucepan. Bring to a boil over medium-high heat. Stir in the apple, onion, and bell pepper. Reduce the heat and simmer, uncovered, 10 to 15 minutes or until it thickens slightly. Stir it often. Allow to cool, then pour into sterilized glass bottles. A glass jar that used to contain mayonnaise or juice works real well. Refrigerate for up to 2 weeks.

Makes 3 cups

Variation: To make this sauce a little hotter, add more cayenne pepper to taste, approximately another ¼ to ½ teaspoon. Be careful; a little cayenne goes a long way.

INGREDIENTS:

- 1 cup ketchup (I use Hunt's)
- ⅔ cup seasoned rice vinegar
- ½ cup apple juice or cider
- ¼ cup apple cider vinegar
- ½ cup packed brown sugar
- ¼ cup soy sauce or Worcestershire sauce
- 2 teaspoons prepared yellow mustard
- ¾ teaspoon garlic powder
- ¼ teaspoon ground white pepper
- ¼ teaspoon cayenne
- ⅓ cup bacon bits, ground in a spice grinder
- ⅓ cup peeled and grated apple
- ⅓ cup grated onion
- 2 teaspoons grated green bell pepper

Photo: Luke Adams

Simple Tailgate Dry Ribs

Trim the spareribs (or have your butcher do it for you), and rub both sides of the ribs with the dry rub mixture, being sure to get all surfaces, and work it into the meat. Put the ribs in a shallow dish or zip-top bag and refrigerate overnight.

Preheat grill for indirect cooking.

Place the ribs on the grill, meat side down, on the hot side of the grill and sear until grill marks are on the meat (5–10 minutes). Move the ribs to the cool side of the grill and close the cover. Cook for 1 ½–2 hours, turning every 20–30 minutes.

Serves 6–8.

INGREDIENTS:

5 to 6 pounds spareribs

½ cup spice dry rub (recipe follows)

SPICE RUB

3 tablespoons chili powder

2 tablespoons freshly ground black pepper

2 tablespoons Spanish paprika

2 teaspoons cayenne red pepper

1 teaspoon garlic salt

Spice Rub: Mix the ingredients together in bowl and store in a jar or zip-top bag. Yield: about ½ cup.

Blue Burger

Preheat grill to medium.

Combine first three ingredients in a bowl. Divide ground beef into four equal parts and form into patties. Dig a small hole in the center of each patty and fill with a pile of blue cheese crumbles. Form the patty around the cheese.

Grill patties, flipping once, until cooked to desired doneness. Serve with your favorite burger fixings.

Serves 4.

INGREDIENTS:

1 ½ pounds ground beef

1 small onion, finely chopped

Salt and pepper, to taste

½ pound crumbled blue cheese

Photo: Jon Brower

Rib Eyes with Blue Cheese Butter

In a bowl combine all ingredients for the spice rub and mix well. Rub the mixture on all surfaces of the rib eyes, massaging it into the meat until well seasoned. Let meat rest 30 minutes or refrigerate up to overnight.

In a separate bowl mix the butter and cream cheese. Then add the jalapeno sauce and lemon juice. Fold in the remaining ingredients and refrigerate until ready to use.

Preheat grill to high heat.

Place steaks on the grill and cook for 5–8 minutes on each side or until done to your taste. Remove from the grill and top with the Blue Cheese Butter before serving.

Serves 4.

INGREDIENTS:

4 rib eyes

Spice Rub

4 tablespoons kosher salt

2 tablespoons paprika

1 tablespoon pepper

1 ½ teaspoons onion powder

1 ½ teaspoons garlic powder

1 ½ teaspoons cayenne pepper

½ teaspoon coriander–cumin

½ teaspoon turmeric

Blue Cheese Butter

½ cup butter, softened

1 pack (3 ounces) cream cheese, softened

2 teaspoons jalapeno pepper sauce

Juice of 1 ½ lemons

4 slices bacon, cooked and crumbled

1 teaspoon sniped fresh chives

1 cup crumbled blue cheese

Butterscotch Brownies

Preheat oven to 350° F.

Combine flour, packing powder, and salt in a medium bowl and set aside. In a mixing bowl, beat together butter, brown sugar, and vanilla extract until creamy. Beat the eggs into the mixture, and then gradually add the flour mixture and ¾ of the butterscotch morsels. Spread into an ungreased 13 x 9-inch baking pan and sprinkle remaining morsels on top.

Bake 30–40 minutes until a toothpick or knife inserted in the center comes out clean.

Yield: 3–4 dozen.

INGREDIENTS:

2 ¼ cups all purpose flour

1 teaspoon baking powder

¼ teaspoon salt

1 cup butter, softened

1 ¾ cup brown sugar, packed

1 tablespoon vanilla extract

2 eggs

1 11 ounce-package Nestle Tollhouse Butterscotch morsels, divided

Flourless Chocolate Cake

Preheat the oven to 350°F.

Butter a 9-inch springform pan.

Melt the chocolate and set aside. Whisk the egg yolks with the sugar in a mixing bowl until light yellow in color. Whisk in a little of the melted chocolate into the egg yolk mixture. Then add the rest of the chocolate mixture. (Be sure not to add all of the melted chocolate at once or it may begin to cook the eggs. That's a bad thing.)

Beat the egg whites in a mixing bowl until stiff peaks form and fold into the chocolate mixture. Pour into the prepared pan and bake 20–25 minutes until the cake is set and a toothpick inserted into the cake comes out with moist crumbs on it. Let stand 10–15 minutes before removing the mold.

Top with whipped cream and serve.

Serves 6–8.

INGREDIENTS:

1 pound bittersweet chocolate, chopped into small pieces

1 stick unsalted butter

9 large eggs, separated

¾ cup granulated sugar, plus

1 tablespoon

Whipped cream

Top 5 NFL Tailgating Stadiums

It's hard to definitively say what five stadiums host the best tailgates around the NFL. After all, there are more than five places that throw a great party, and it's your friends that truly make a tailgate great. But these five would make most anyone's list.

1. Kansas City Chiefs

This is one of my favorite places to tailgate. First of all, there are about 20,000 parking spaces at Arrowhead Stadium; that's one way to get a tailgate party started. Next, the parking lot is a sea of red—everyone is spirited and wears their colors. Then there's the barbecue. The aroma is intoxicating, and once you've eaten a couple of plates of it you'll be adding your name to the waiting list for season tickets here.

2. Green Bay Packers

You know tailgating has to be special outside the frozen tundra of Lambeau Field. (You heard that NFL voice in your head while reading that, didn't you?) The stadium basically sits in a neighborhood, so early in the morning the chairs and grills start to pop up in driveways and lawns across the area. During the day the party moves to the parking lot, and it stays there for hours after the game. These are some of the most loyal fans you'll find, too.

3. Pittsburgh Steelers

There's a lot of tradition in these parking lots. Okay, not in these parking lots (Heinz Field has been around only since 2001), but these fans tailgated in the lots around Three Rivers Stadium for generations and that tradition continues. Plenty of brats and sausage on the grill, too. Here you'll find some of the league's most fanatic fans turn pregame into a great party even if it's freezing and snowing.

4. Houston Texans

Although the new kid on the block, these tailgaters come to compete. And the competition is often for the best barbeque in the parking lot. Parking spaces in parts of the lot are filled with fans cooking on converted trucks, trailers, and pit smokers doing it up right. The Texans also did it up right when they built Reliant Stadium, creating parking lots accommodating to tailgaters.

5. Denver Broncos

The Broncos are known for their home field advantage, and it begins in the parking lot. Maybe it's the altitude, but you have rabid fans who compete in weekly, themed contests, show up early to grab the best spots, and have everything from beef to fish on the grill.

WHERE TO TAILGATE

At most stadiums tailgating isn't as easy as pulling up before kickoff, grabbing a parking space, and tapping a keg. Actually, most places won't let you have kegs. There're rules against that, among other things.

That's what this chapter is all about—what you can do, can't do, and tips for doing it at every NFL and NCAA Division I-A stadium in the country. I've also included some stadium and team information, so you'll fit right in, even if it's a road trip. After all, you'll look pretty silly being the only one not to know that the University of Idaho is the Vandals.

At the time I sent this to the printer all of the information was correct. But things can change; so if you have any questions or want to double-check a detail you can call the numbers listed for each team to learn the latest.

Photo: Bruce Newman

Venue Guide Key

The team pages in this chapter will help you navigate the parking lots at every NFL and NCAA Division I-A stadium. You can use the icons below for a quick reference but I've also included more details and some facts and tid-bits about the teams and some of their great players.

 Decorations are allowed, excluding banners and signs that are advertising services or goods.

 Alcohol is permitted for those of legal drinking age.

 Grills or cookers are permitted for noncommercial use only.

 Parking is more than $50 per day for cars or larger vehicles.

 Parking is between $30 and $50 per day for cars or larger vehicles.

 Parking is no more than $30 per day for any vehicle.

 RVs may park overnight before or after the game.

 Number of hours you can tailgate before game. Times exceeding 4 hours are included in "4" icon.

 Number of hours you may remain after the event. Usually this includes tailgating, but read the entry to be sure.

 RVs, limos, and other oversized vehicles are allowed.

 Tents may be erected.

 Tables, chairs, and other tailgating furniture are allowed.

 Venue offers visible security presence in parking and tailgating areas.

 Venue offers at least one paved parking lot.

Shuttle service available from parking or tailgating areas to the event and back again.

Note: On the college football team pages an asterisk (*) indicates a shared or contested college football national championship.

Arizona Cardinals

Franchise Colors: Cardinal Red, Black, White

Stadium: University of Phoenix

Capacity: 73,000

Surface: Roll Out Grass

Opened: 2006

Phone: (602) 379-0102

Mascot Name: Big Red

Cheerleading Squad Name: Arizona Cardinals Cheerleaders

Super Bowl Championships: None

Glendale, Arizona

Radio Partner: KTAR 620 AM

Hall of Fame Members:

Charles W. Bidwill Sr.

Guy Chamberlin

Jimmy Conzelman

Dan Dierdorf

John (Paddy) Driscoll

Walt Kiesling

Earl (Curly) Lambeau

Dick (Night Train) Lane

Ollie Matson

Don Maynard

Ernie Nevers

Jackie Smith

Jim Thorpe

Charley Trippi

Larry Wilson

No single-game RV parking available at Sportsman's Park on game day, season tickets only. Visiting RVs use Lot H on 91st Avenue, south of Kellis High School. Get there early; there are a limited number of spaces. RVs must already have valid oversized vehicle hangtag–no paid parking available game day. Only gas or propane grills allowed. One space per vehicle, one 10 x 10-foot tent per vehicle. Public drunkenness not tolerated.

Shuttle info: Shuttles free from Lot H. Service starts 2 hours before game, ends 1 hour after game's end.

Atlanta Falcons

Franchise Colors: Red, Black, White, Silver

Stadium: Georgia Dome

Capacity: 71,228

Surface: FieldTurf

Opened: 1992

Phone: (404) 223-8000 (Office), (404) 223-8444 (Operations)

Mascot Name: Freddie Falcon

Cheerleading Squad Name: Atlanta Falcons Cheerleaders

Super Bowl Championships: None

Atlanta, Georgia

Radio Partner: WZGC 92.9 FM

> **Hall of Fame Members:**
> Eric Dickerson
> Tommy McDonald

RVs park in Yellow Lot on corner of Simpson and Northside Drive. There are many independent lots within walking distance. Most lots have no stringent restrictions; no overnight parking. One new feature: Tag-A-Kid arm bracelets available at any Dome Service Center. Bracelets list child's and parent's names, contact number, and seat location.

Shuttle info: Atlanta's public transportation system drops off fans from numerous locations. Season ticket holders use MARTA Breeze passes.

Baltimore Ravens

Franchise Colors: Black, Purple, Metallic Gold, White

Stadium: M&T Bank

Capacity: 69,084

Surface: Sportexe MomentumTurf

Opened: 1998

Phone: (410) 261-RAVE, (410) 347-9330 (Central Parking)

Mascot Names: Edgar, Allen, and Poe

Cheerleading Squad Name: Baltimore Raven Cheerleaders

Super Bowl Championships: (1)–XXXV

Hall of Fame Members: None

Baltimore, Maryland

Radio Partners: WBAL 1090 AM, WIYY 97.9 FM

RVs parking in Lot J, $100. Advance parking, call Central Parking number. Day of game RV parking sold as available. No overnight parking. Car park in private lots, within walking distance. No cooking within 2 feet of vehicle. No other real restrictions, but public drunkenness or obnoxious behavior won't be tolerated. Visit Raven's Walk for pregame fun, sponsored activities. You'll be frisked upon entering stadium. Really.

Shuttle info: Shuttles start three hours prior to game time. Shuttles run from Blackstone Lot at World Fair Park, also from Coliseum, Old City and Market Square area of downtown, $4 per person, round-trip. Shuttles also running from Farragut High School, $10 per person round-trip.

Buffalo Bills

Franchise Colors: Dark Navy, Red, Royal Blue, Nickel, White

Stadium: Ralph Wilson

Capacity: 73,967

Surface: AstroPlay Turf

Opened: 1973

Phone: (716) 648-1800, (877) BB-TICKS

Mascot Name: Billy the Buffalo

Cheerleading Squad Name: Buffalo Jills

Super Bowl Championships: None

Orchard Park, New York

Radio Partners: WEDG 103.3 FM, WGRF 96.9 FM

RVs can arrive Friday between 6 and 9 p.m., $30, or Saturday 8 a.m., $25. RV parking lots located along One Bills Drive; RVs should park in Lot Drive 6 or Lot Drive 7; cars park in Drive 1 through Drive 7. Tailgate in front or behind your vehicle only. Extinguish all flames and grills before entering or leaving stadium. Vehicles may occupy only one parking space.

Shuttle info: Parking's pretty close. No shuttles needed.

Hall of Fame Members:
Joe Delamielleure
Jim Kelly
Marv Levy
James Lofton
Billy Shaw
O. J. Simpson

Carolina Panthers

Franchise Colors: Black, Panther Blue, Silver, White

Stadium: Bank of America

Capacity: 73,500

Surface: Grass

Opened: 1996

Phone: (704) 358-7000, (704) 376-5559 (EZ Parking)

Mascot Name: Sir Purr

Cheerleading Squad Name: Top Cats

Super Bowl Championships: None

Charlotte, North Carolina

Radio Partners: WBT 1110 AM, WBT 99.3 FM

> **Hall of Fame Members:**
> Reggie White

All RV parking handled by EZ Parking. EZ has several locations ranging from $50 to $125 (depending on location). Call a week in advance; they'll fax you a map of best available locations. When available, extra space for your tailgate can also be rented. No grills within 25 feet of building (except parking deck) and 10 feet of vehicle.

Shuttle info: All parking within 1/2 mile of the stadium. Shuttles not needed.

Chicago Bears

Franchise Colors: Dark Navy, Orange, White

Stadium: Soldier Field

Capacity: 63,000

Surface: Grass

Opened: 1924

Phone: (847) 615-BEAR (Ticket Office), (888) 79-BEARS (Fan Services), (312) 583-9153 (Parking Hotline)

Mascot Name: Staley

Cheerleading Squad Name: None

Super Bowl Championships: (1)–XX

Chicago, Illinois

Radio Partners: WBBM 780 AM

RVs and bigger vehicles park at Adler Planetarium, first-come, first-served, $85. No overnight parking. No tents or canopies of any size; no ad banners or displays; no political campaigning or protesting; no tethered blimps, balloons, or oversized inflatables; no weapons, fireworks, or disorderly conduct; no saving spaces or in/out privileges. Stay inside your space. Otherwise, have fun!

Shuttle info: East Monroe Street garage and Millennium Garage have free shuttle service starting 3 hours before game, until 2 hours after game's end.

Hall of Fame Members:
Doug Atkins
George Blanda
Dick Butkus
Guy Chamberlin
George Connor
Jimmy Conzelman
Mike Ditka
John (Paddy) Driscoll
Jim Finks
Dan Fortmann
Bill George
Harold (Red) Grange
George Halas
Dan Hampton
Ed Healey
Bill Hewitt
Stan Jones
Walt Kiesling
Bobby Layne
Sid Luckman
William Roy (Link) Lyman
George McAfee
George Musso
Bronko Nagurski
Alan Page
Walter Payton
Gale Sayers
Mike Singletary
Joe Stydahar
George Trafton
Clyde (Bulldog) Turner

Cincinnati Bengals

Franchise Colors: Black, Orange, White

Stadium: Paul Brown

Capacity: 65,352

Surface: FieldTurf

Opened: 2000

Phone: (513) 455-4800, (513) 455-8383 (Ticket Office), (513) 946-8100 (Central Parking)

Mascot Name: Who Dey

Cheerleading Squad Name: Ben-gals

Super Bowl Championships: None

Cincinnati, Ohio

Radio Partners: WCKY 1530 AM, WLW 700 AM, WOFX 92.5 FM

> **Hall of Fame Members:**
> Charlie Joiner Anthony Muñoz

Parking available for cars, RVs, and larger vehicles at various lots and prices, but none of them is cheap. No overnight parking. Single-game lots available north of Third Street. Stay past 1 a.m. and you'll be towed. No items restricted; prefer charcoal grills. Visit the Jungle Zone for pregame fun.

Shuttle info: Use public transportation. Drop off area for Metro is located under Second Street in the transit center. Drop off area for TANK (Transit Authority of Northern Kentucky) is located on Central Avenue heading south.

Cleveland Browns

Franchise Colors: Brown, Orange, White

Stadium: Cleveland Browns

Capacity: 73,200

Surface: Grass

Opened: 1999

Phone: (216) 367-7912 (AMPCO Parking)

Mascot Names: Trapper, T. D., Chomps, and C. B.

Super Bowl Championships: None

Cleveland, Ohio

Radio Partners: WMMS 100.7 FM, WTAM 1100 AM

Stadium doesn't offer parking. Best bet is nearby Port of Cleveland parking lot. Can prepay through AMPCO Parking. RVs can park in garages, and can park in open lots the day before until the morning after the game. No open alcohol containers. Buzzard Barking Lot has pregame entertainment.

Shuttle info: Cleveland's RTA rapid system Waterfront line stops at Cleveland Stadium and can be accessed from Public Square.

Hall of Fame Members:
Doug Atkins
Jim Brown
Paul Brown
Willie Davis
Len Dawson
Joe DeLamielleure
Len Ford
Frank Gatski
Otto Graham
Lou Groza
Henry Jordan
Leroy Kelly
Dante Lavelli
Mike McCormack
Tommy McDonald
Bobby Mitchell
Marion Motley
Ozzie Newsome
Paul Warfield
Bill Willis

Dallas Cowboys

Franchise Colors: Navy, Metallic Silver Blue, White

Stadium: Texas

Capacity: 65,639

Surface: Artificial Turf

Opened: 1972

Mascot Name: Rowdy

Cheerleading Squad Name: Dallas Cowboy Cheerleaders

Super Bowl Championships: (5)—VI, XII, XXVII, XXVIII, XXX

Irving, Texas

Radio Partners: KBDN 93.3 FM, KTCK 1310 AM

RVs park in lot on Texas Plaza. No overnight parking. Tailgating allowed at all Texas Stadium Parking Lots. Occupy only as many spaces as you have parking passes. If you bring a grill on a trailer, you must have additional spot for trailer. Ash cans and trash cans are located throughout the parking lots for your use. Use safety in all tailgating activities.

Shuttle info: Sorry, shuttle service no longer provided.

Hall of Fame Members:

Herb Adderley
Troy Aikman
Lance Alworth
Mike Ditka
Tony Dorsett
Forrest Gregg
Tom Landry
Bob Lilly
Tommy McDonald
Mel Renfro
Tex Schramm
Jackie Smith
Roger Staubach
Randy White
Rayfield Wright

Denver Broncos

Franchise Colors: Broncos Navy, Orange, White

Stadium: INVESCO Field at Mile High

Capacity: 76,125

Surface: Grass

Opened: 2001

Mascot Name: Miles

Cheerleading Squad Name: Denver Broncos Cheerleaders

Super Bowl Championships: (2)–XXXII, XXXIII

Denver, Colorado

Radio Partner: KOA 850 AM

> **Hall of Fame Members:**
> Willie Brown
> Tony Dorsett
> John Elway

Single-game RV parking on south side of Colfax Ave in Lots M, $30 per space used, and Lots N and P, $20 per space. RVs will use 2 spaces. No glass bottles, kegs, open fires, saving spaces, unauthorized vehicles, or blocking pedestrian traffic. No advertising, promoting, or selling anything without permission. Coal disposal bins provided. Broncos host tailgating contests with themes for different games.

Shuttle info: Twenty-eight free Park & Ride lots along Federal Boulevard and Market Street Station. First shuttle starts 60 to 150 minutes before kickoff. Last bus leaves stadium 45 minutes after game ends. Lots are free; shuttles are $3 round trip.

Detroit Lions

School Colors: Honolulu Blue, Silver, Black, White

Stadium: Ford Field

Capacity: 65,000

Surface: FieldTurf

Opened: 2002

Phone: (800) 616-ROAR, (313) 831-5236 (Handy, Mobile), (586) 784-1005 (Park Right), (313) 832-8154 (Eastern Market), (313) 967-1666 (Parking Department)

Mascot Name: Roary

Cheerleading Squad Name: None

Super Bowl Championships: None

Detroit, Michigan

Radio Partners: WKRK 97.1 FM

Hall of Fame Members:
Lem Barney
Jack Christiansen
Earl (Dutch) Clark
Lou Creekmur
Bill Dudley
Frank Gatski
John Henry Johnson
Dick (Night Train) Lane
Yale Lary
Bobby Layne
Ollie Matson
Hugh McElhenny
Barry Sanders
Joe Schmidt
Doak Walker
Alex Wojciechowicz

All public parking handled by private companies; each has its own rules. The Lions recommend parking in the Eastern Market since there's a shuttle. Get spaces in advance from city's Parking Department.

Shuttle info: Shuttles drop off and pick up guests on Adams Street, between Witherell and John R. This is not a parking area! Drop-offs begin 2 hours before game. Pickups begin at start of fourth quarter. The Detroit People Mover's (part of Detroit's public transit system) nearest stops to stadium are Greektown, Broadway, and Grand Circus Stations. Fare is $.50.

Green Bay Packers

Franchise Colors: Dark Green, Gold, White

Stadium: Lambeau Field

Capacity: 72,515

Surface: Kentucky Bluegrass

Opened: 1957

Mascot Name: None

Cheerleading Squad Name: None

Super Bowl Championships: (3)–I, II, XXXI

Green Bay, Wisconsin

Radio Partners: WTMJ 620 AM

RVs can't park at stadium. Overnight RV parking 3 blocks away, $60. Same parking, for day only, $50. Most lots have coal disposal bins. Keep everything inside your space. Some downtown lots sell extra space, some don't. Best bet for cars is to park on residential streets. Some home owners sell space. No open fires!

Shuttle info: Parking's close enough that special shuttles aren't needed.

Hall of Fame Members:

Herb Adderley
Tony Canadeo
Willie Davis
Len Ford
Forrest Gregg
Ted Hendricks
Arnie Herber
Clarke Hinkle
Paul Hornung
Robert (Cal) Hubbard
Don Hutson
Henry Jordan
Walt Kiesling
Earl (Curly) Lambeau
James Lofton
Vince Lombardi
John (Blood) McNally
Mike Michalske
Ray Nitschke
Jim Ringo
Bart Starr
Jan Stenerud
Jim Taylor
Emlen Tunnell
Reggie White
Willie Wood

Houston Texans

Franchise Colors: Deep Steel Blue, Battle Red, Liberty White

Stadium: Reliant

Capacity: 69,500

Surface: Grass

Opened: 2002

Phone: (832) 667-2000, (877) NFL-2002

Mascot Name: Toro the Bull

Cheerleading Squad Name: Houston Texans Cheerleaders

Super Bowl Championships: None

Hall of Fame Members: None

Houston, Texas

Radio Partners: 990-AM WNOX, KILT 610 AM, KILT 100.3 FM

Most stadium parking for season ticket holders. Single-game RVs park in Maroon Lot. Call Ticketmaster for parking passes, $15 each. RVs need 2 or 3 passes. No overnight parking. Towed cookers need additional hangtag. Fans can purchase extra hangtag for additional tailgating area (call -2002 extension for hangtags). No saving spaces for pals. Stadium tailgating limited to parking spot and space behind vehicle. Don't block traffic in driving lane. Put everything away before kickoff. No large balloons, golf carts, or scooters. Fire extinguishers required; no lighter fluid for charcoal grills. If Maroon lot full, park in nearby RV parks: South Main RV Park or All Star RV Resort.

Shuttle info: Shuttles start three hours prior to game time. Shuttles run from Blackstone Lot at World Fair Park, also from Coliseum, Old City and Market Square area of downtown, $4 per person, round-trip. Shuttles also running from Farragut High School, $10 per person round-trip.

Indianapolis Colts

Franchise Colors: Royal Blue, White

Stadium: RCA Dome

Capacity: 56,127

Surface: FieldTurf

Opened: 1984

Phone: (317) 636-8552, (317) 262-3400 (RCA Dome)

Mascot Names: Spike and Spirit

Cheerleading Squad Name: Indianapolis Colts Cheerleaders

Super Bowl Championships: (2)–V, XLI

Indianapolis, Indiana

Radio Partner: WFBQ 94.7

Tailgating in South Lot immediately south of RCA Dome. You'll be directed to a spot. Hook ups available for RVs; no night-before parking, but you can leave the day after. No open fires. Pregame fun at C.P. Morgan Competition Center.

Shuttle info: Use Indianapolis's IndyGo Blue Line route; it stops at Convention Center side of RCA Dome. The Blue Line runs every 10 minutes from 10 a.m. to 10 p.m., 7 days a week. Fare is $.25.

Hall of Fame Members:
Raymond Berry
Eric Dickerson
Art Donovan
Weeb Ewbank
Ted Hendricks
John Mackey
Gino Marchetti
Lenny Moore
Jim Parker
Joe Perry
Don Shula
Johnny Unitas

Jacksonville Jaguars

Franchise Colors: Teal, Black, Gold, White

Stadium: Alltel

Capacity: 73,000

Surface: Grass

Opened: 1995

Mascot Name: Jaxson De Ville

Cheerleading Squad Name: Jacksonville Jaguars Cheerleaders

Super Bowl Championships: None

Hall of Fame Members: None

Jacksonville, Florida

Radio Partners: WJGL 96.9 FM, WOKV 690 AM

Few stadium spaces for visitors; park in city and take shuttles. All must call to reserve a spot. A parking pass will be mailed to you. RVs have two lots; call ahead to get a space. No overnight parking. Call (904) 353-1126 to reserve a spot in the Tailgate Lot; for serious tailgaters, although more expensive. No open fires. Pepsi Plaza has pregame entertainment and fun.

Shuttle info: Jacksonville Transportation Authority has stadium shuttle service with free parking in several downtown locations. Service starts 2 hours before game, ends 1 hour after game's end.

Kansas City Chiefs

Franchise Colors: Red, Gold, White

Stadium: Arrowhead

Capacity: 79,451

Surface: Grass

Opened: 1972

Phone: (816) 920-4382

Mascot Name: K.C. Wolf

Cheerleading Squad Name: Kansas City Chiefs Cheerleaders

Super Bowl Championships: (1)–IV

Kansas City, Missouri

Radio Partners: KCFX 101.1 FM

Hall of Fame Members:
Marcus Allen
Bobby Bell
Junious (Buck) Buchanan
Len Dawson
Lamar Hunt
Willie Lanier
Marv Levy
Joe Montana
Warren Moon
Jan Stenerud
Hank Stram
Mike Webster

Single-game RVs park in Lots L and N. RV parking varies $90 to $150, depending on game, length of stay, and any tow vehicles. In all lots, oversized vehicles park in back of lot or in grass. Vehicles pulling a trailer of any kind charged for extra parking space, must park in grass. No scooters, ATVs, motorcycles, golf carts, or other motorized units. No open fires, no camping tents, no pets. Do not dump waste.

Shuttle info: Kansas City Metro Chief's Express carries fans from downtown to game $8 in advance, $10 game day. Service starts 2 1/2 hours before game. After game, busses leave promptly.

Miami Dolphins

Franchise Colors: Aqua, Coral, Navy, White

Stadium: Dolphin

Capacity: 75,540

Surface: Grass

Opened: 1987

Phone: (305) 623-6100

Mascot Name: T.D.

Cheerleading Squad Name: Miami Dolphins Cheerleaders

Super Bowl Championships: (2)–VII, VIII

Miami, Florida

Radio Partners: WAXY 790 AM, WBGG 105.9 FM

Hall of Fame Members:
Nick Buoniconti
Larry Csonka
Bob Griese
Jim Langer
Larry Little
Dan Marino
Don Shula
Dwight Stephenson
Paul Warfield

Single-game RVs park in northwest corner Lot 8, next to cash lot. Parking is $50. Season ticket holders always have first dibs on all parking. Tailgate directly behind your vehicle; don't block lane. Grills are fine; campfires aren't. Extinguish hot coals before leaving area. Put cold coals into trash bag; place in garbage bin. Keep emergency lanes clear. Use Lost Little Linebackers wrist tag program to help children find their seats when lost.

Shuttle info: Shuttles start three hours prior to game time. Shuttles run from Blackstone Lot at World Fair Park, also from Coliseum, Old City and Market Square area of downtown, $4 per person, round-trip. Shuttles also running from Farragut High School, $10 per person round-trip.

Minnesota Vikings

Franchise Colors: Purple, Gold, White, Black

Stadium: Hubert H. Humphrey Metrodome

Capacity: 64,121

Surface: FieldTurf

Opened: 1982

Mascot Name: Ragnar

Cheerleading Squad Name: Minnesota Vikings Cheerleaders

Super Bowl Championships: None

Minneapolis, Minnesota

Radio Partners: KFAN 1130 AM, KQQL 107.9 FM

You wanna tailgate? Go to Rapid Park, behind Target Center at 600 3rd Avenue N. RVs pay $40; cars pay $20. No overnight parking; no open fires. Don't wear Packers colors unless you're okay with getting razzed. Local food specialty is fried asparagus. Minneapolis offers lots of fun—go exploring!

Shuttle info: Park at Rapid Park and get voucher for free bus service, rail transportation to and from Metrodome. Service runs to and from stadium every 10 minutes.

Hall of Fame Members:
Dave Casper
Carl Eller
Jim Finks
Bud Grant
Paul Krause
Jim Langer
Hugh McElhenny
Warren Moon
Alan Page
Jan Stenerud
Fran Tarkenton
Ron Yary

New England Patriots

Franchise Colors: Nautical Blue, Red, New Century Silver, White

Stadium: Gillette

Capacity: 68,000

Surface: FieldTurf

Opened: 2002

Phone: (508) 543-1776

Mascot Name: Pat

Cheerleading Squad Name: New England Patriots Cheerleaders

Super Bowl Championships: (3)–XXXVI, XXXVIII, XXXIX

Foxborough, Massachusetts

Radio Partners: WBCN 104.1 FM

> **Hall of Fame Members:**
> Nick Buoniconti
> John Hannah
> Mike Haynes

RVs $125, cars $35, buses $200. Arrive early to get good spaces. RVs park in designated area; enter at P10. Limos enter P2 or P6. Buses or disabled at P5 or P6. Many items prohibited; check gillettestadium.com for updated list.

Shuttle info: Parking is close; no shuttles needed.

New Orleans Saints

Franchise Colors: Old Gold, Black, White

Stadium: Louisiana Superdome

Capacity: 70,200

Surface: Sportexe Momentum Turf

Opened: 1975

Mascot Name: Gumbo

Cheerleading Squad Name: Saintsations

Super Bowl Championships: None

New Orleans, Louisiana

Radio Partner: WWL 870 AM

Hall of Fame Members:
Doug Atkins
Earl Campbell
Jim Finks
Hank Stram
Jim Taylor

RVs can park at surface lot on Girod Street, $50. Cars can park at Gate A garage, $25. No tailgating in garages, of course. RVs can tailgate, but must use "flatbed"-style grill (like a griddle); no open flame grills allowed. Extra spots may be available for purchase. Call ahead of time. Multiple parking in public pay lots on side streets surrounding the Superdome. Get here up to 5 hours before game; remember, the later you come, the longer you walk.

Shuttle info: Use public transportation.

New York Giants

Franchise Colors: Dark Blue, Red, White, Gray

Stadium: Giants

Capacity: 80,062

Surface: FieldTurf

Opened: 1976

Phone: (201) 460-4187

Mascot Name: None

Cheerleading Squad Name: None

Super Bowl Championships: (2)–XXI, XXV

East Rutherford, New Jersey

Radio Partner: WFAN 660 AM

Parking surrounds stadium. No grilling on sidewalks or next to buildings; no open fires, ball playing, or Frisbee tossing. No overnight parking. Dispose of charcoal safely.

Shuttle info: Busses run between stadium and Port Authority Bus Terminal in Manhattan.

Hall of Fame Members:

Morris (Red) Badgro
Roosevelt Brown
Harry Carson
Larry Csonka
Ray Flaherty
Benny Friedman
Frank Gifford
Joe Guyon
Mel Hein
Wilbur (Pete) Henry
Arnie Herber
Robert (Cal) Hubbard
Sam Huff
Alphonse (Tuffy) Leemans
Tim Mara
Wellington Mara
Don Maynard
Hugh McElhenny
Steve Owen
Andy Robustelli
Ken Strong
Fran Tarkenton
Lawrence Taylor
Jim Thorpe
Y. A. Tittle
Emlen Tunnell
Arnie Weinmeister

New York Jets

Franchise Colors: Hunter Green, White

Stadium: The Meadowlands

Capacity: 80,062

Surface: FieldTurf

Opened: 1976

Phone: (201) 460-4187

Mascot Name: None

Cheerleading Squad Name: None

Super Bowl Championships: (1)–III

East Rutherford, New Jersey

Radio Partners: WABC 770 AM, WEPN 1050 AM, WADO 1280 AM (Spanish)

Hall of Fame Members:
Weeb Ewbank
Ronnie Lott
Don Maynard
Joe Namath
John Riggins

Parking surrounds stadium. No grilling on sidewalks or next to buildings; no open fires, ball playing, or Frisbee tossing. No overnight parking. Dispose of charcoal safely. Four Oasis stations have different themes, alumni, gear, and more. Each also has a beer garden, food, and seats 250.

Shuttle info: Buses run between stadium and Port Authority Bus Terminal in Manhattan.

Oakland Raiders

Franchise Colors: Silver, Black, White

Stadium: McAfee Coliseum

Capacity: 63,150

Surface: Bluegrass

Opened: 1966

Mascot Name: None

Cheerleading Squad Name: The Raiderettes

Super Bowl Championships: (3)–XII, XV, XVIII

Oakland, California

Radio Partner: KSFO 560 AM

RVs park in specific lot, $50. No overnight parking. Many do so across the street a day or more before the game. No kegs, no glass. All charcoal must be extinguished, disposed of in fireproof containers provided, or taken home when you leave. Stadium serious about banned items.

Shuttle info: Use city, county public transit options.

Hall of Fame Members:

Marcus Allen

Fred Biletnikoff

George Blanda

Bob (Boomer) Brown

Willie Brown

Dave Casper

Al Davis

Eric Dickerson

Mike Haynes

Ted Hendricks

James Lofton

Howie Long

Ronnie Lott

John Madden

Ron Mix

Jim Otto

Art Shell

Gene Upshaw

Philadelphia Eagles

Franchise Colors: Midnight Green, Black, Charcoal, Silver, White

Stadium: Lincoln Financial Field

Capacity: 68,534

Surface: Grass

Opened: 2003

Phone: (215) 339-6757

Mascot Name: Swoop

Cheerleading Squad Name: Philadelphia Eagles Cheerleaders

Super Bowl Championships: None

Philadelphia, Pennsylvania

Radio Partner: FREE 94.1 FM

All parking within 3-block radius of stadium. RVs pay for number of spots used. No overnight parking; stay within your space. No tailgating north of Pattison Avenue. Visit Eagles Ultimate Tailgate Party; you'll need a ticket.

Shuttle info: No shuttles, but subway is close by if you're coming from downtown.

Hall of Fame Members:
Chuck Bednarik
Bert Bell
Bob (Boomer) Brown
Mike Ditka
Bill Hewitt
Sonny Jurgensen
James Lofton
Ollie Matson
Tommy McDonald
Earle (Greasy) Neale
Pete Pihos
Jim Ringo
Norm Van Brocklin
Steve Van Buren
Reggie White
Alex Wojciechowicz

Pittsburgh Steelers

Franchise Colors: Black, Gold, White

Stadium: Heinz Field

Capacity: 64,451

Surface: Grass

Opened: 2001

Phone: (412) 323-4455

Mascot Name: None

Cheerleading Squad Name: None

Super Bowl Championships: (5)–IX, X, XIII, XIV, XL

Pittsburgh, Pennsylvania

Radio Partners: WBGG 970 AM, WDVE 102.5 FM

Lots open 5 hours before game; parking $25 to $35 per space–RVs need between 2 and 4 spaces. Downtown garages only $5, but no grilling inside a garage. No overnight parking or sleeping tents. One space per vehicle (except for RVs who need more). Take home whatever furniture you bring with you. A good bet: use downtown garages and lots in the Golden Triangle area and take advantage of excellent shuttle service.

Shuttle info: Golden Triangle shuttle only $1.25 each way.

Hall of Fame Members:
Bert Bell
Mel Blount
Terry Bradshaw
Len Dawson
Bill Dudley
(Mean) Joe Greene
Jack Ham
Franco Harris
Robert (Cal) Hubbard
John Henry Johnson
Walt Kiesling
Jack Lambert
Bobby Layne
John (Blood) McNally
Marion Motley
Chuck Noll
Art Rooney
Dan Rooney
John Stallworth
Ernie Stautner
Lynn Swann
Mike Webster

San Diego Chargers

Franchise Colors: Navy, Gold, White

Stadium: Qualcomm

Capacity: 71,000

Surface: Grass

Opened: 1967

Phone: (619) 641-3100, (619) 281-6316, (619) 281-PARK

Mascot Name: None

Cheerleading Squad Name: Charger Girls

Super Bowl Championships: None

San Diego, California

Radio Partner: KIOZ 105.3 FM

Hall of Fame Members:
Lance Alworth
Dan Fouts
Sid Gillman
Charlie Joiner
David (Deacon) Jones
Larry Little
John Mackey
Ron Mix
Johnny Unitas
Kellen Winslow

RVs and oversized vehicles park in designated RV Parking area located in section A3 of parking lot; enter Gate 1 from San Diego Mission Rd. Overflow parking for RVs in section A2 and A4 if necessary. Call -7275 extension for reservation. Can purchase up to 2 companion spots to park car, $20 each. RVs not allowed in inner or outer parking areas. Tailgates with catered food service or with a keg must provide proof of liability insurance; obtain permit from Qualcomm Stadium Manager. Kids' I.D. bracelets, marked with seat locations, available at all Guest Services locations.

Shuttle info: City's Chargers Express Bus serves from 5 convenient locations. Round trip fare is $10 or $6 one-way (exact change required). City trolley, county bus service also provides rides.

San Francisco 49ers

Franchise Colors: Cardinal Red, Metallic Gold, Black, White

Stadium: Monster Park

Capacity: 69,400

Surface: Bluegrass

Opened: 1960

Phone: (415) 656-4949

Mascot Name: Sourdough Sam

Cheerleading Squad Name: The Gold Rush

Super Bowl Championships: (5)–XVI, XIX, XXIII, XXIV, XXIX

San Francisco, California

Radio Partners: KNBR 680 AM, KSAN 107.7 FM

> **Hall of Fame Members:**
> Jimmy Johnson
> John Henry Johnson
> Ronnie Lott
> Hugh McElhenny
> Joe Montana
> Leo Nomellini
> Joe Perry
> O. J. Simpson
> Bon St. Clair
> Y. A. Tittle
> Bill Walsh
> Dave Wilcox
> Steve Young

RV Parking $40 per vehicle. RVs, oversized vehicles 17 feet or longer (including self-contained campers) park in RV Lot. Entrance located on corner of Gilman Avenue and Bill Walsh Way. To get there, take Third Street to Gilman Avenue, turn right on Bill Walsh Way. Don't dump coals onto parking surface; use designated receptacles located throughout lots.

Shuttle info: Direct bus service to stadium available on the San Francisco Municipal Railway (MUNI), Santa Clara Valley Transportation Authority, or San Mateo County Transit (Sam Trans) buses.

Seattle Seahawks

Franchise Colors: Pacific Blue, Dark Navy, Bright Green, White

Stadium: Qwest Field

Capacity: 67,000

Surface: FieldTurf

Opened: 2002

Phone: (206) 381-7816, (206) 284-3100 (Diamond Parking)

Mascot Name: Blitz

Cheerleading Squad Name: The Sea Gals

Super Bowl Championships: None

Seattle, Washington

Radio Partner: KIRO 710 AM

Hall of Fame Members:
Carl Eller
Franco Harris
Steve Largent
Warren Moon

Unreserved/overflow RV parking available ($120) on first-come, first-served basis at WOSCO Lot at Railroad Way and Royal Brougham, behind buildings on First Avenue South. (WOSCO is a private lot; call Diamond Parking for updated info.) Overnight parking at WOSCO available, if no big event happening day before, or day after, Seahawks game.

Shuttle info: Washington State Ferry service operates on regular schedule. Over 10 transit routes pass within 3 blocks of sports complex, operating at least every 30 minutes, including weekends.

St. Louis Rams

Franchise Colors: New Century Gold, Millennium Blue, White

Stadium: Edward Jones Dome

Capacity: 66,000

Surface: FieldTurf

Opened: 1995

Phone: (314) 982-7267, (314) 241-7777 ext. 37 (St. Louis Parking Company), (800) 777-0777 (Casino Queen)

Mascot Name: None

Cheerleading Squad Name: St. Louis Rams Cheerleaders

Super Bowl Championships: (1)—XXXIV

St. Louis, Missouri

Radio Partners: KLOU 103.3 FM, KTRS 550 AM

Due to heavy construction/city projects, downtown parking now more complicated, with frequent changes. As of press time, RVs can park in First and Biddle Lot (behind Al's Restaurant) first-come, first-served. No tailgating in Broadway and Locust Lot N. RV-friendly Lot K, at 10th and Cass, no longer in operation. Best bet for single-game RVs: park across river in Casino Queen's RV Park, $23 to $33 per night, with full hookups.

Shuttle info: No Dome shuttles available; not really needed. If parked across town, use public transit. If parked at Casino Queen, ride Metrolink, get off at Convention Center stop, walk last 2 or 3 blocks to Dome.

Hall of Fame Members:
George Allen
Bob (Boomer) Brown
Eric Dickerson
Tom Fears
Bill George
Sid Gillman
Elroy (Crazy Legs) Hirsch
David (Deacon) Jones
Dick (Night Train) Lane
James Lofton
Tom Mack
Ollie Matson
Tommy McDonald
Joe Namath
Merlin Olsen
Dan Reeves
Andy Robustelli
Tex Schramm
Jackie Slater
Norm Van Brocklin
Bob Waterfield
Ron Yary
Jack Youngblood

Tampa Bay Buccaneers

Franchise Colors: Buccaneer Red, Pewter, Black, Orange, White

Stadium: Raymond James

Capacity: 65,657

Surface: Bermuda Grass

Opened: 1998

Phone: (813) 350-6500

Mascot Name: Captain Fear

Cheerleading Squad Name: Tampa Bay Buccaneers Cheerleaders

Super Bowl Championships: (1)–XXXVII

Tampa, Florida

Radio Partners: WDAE 620 AM, WFUS 103.5 FM, WAMA 1550 AM (Spanish)

....
Hall of Fame Members:
Lee Roy Selmon
Steve Young
....

RV parking only in Lots 13 and 14, $50, plus $25 for each additional space taken up by oversized RVs or other extended vehicles. No overnight parking. Stay within your space; no throwing footballs or Frisbees. Check out "pirate ship" Buccaneer Cove. Local tailgating specialty is Cuban sandwiches–*muy bueno!*

Shuttle info: No shuttle service, just taxis.

Tennessee Titans

Franchise Colors: Navy, Titans Blue, White, Red, Silver

Stadium: LP Field

Capacity: 68,800

Surface: Tifsport Bermuda Sod

Opened: 1999

Phone: (615) 565-4000

Mascot Name: T-Rac the Raccoon

Cheerleading Squad Name: Tennessee Titans Cheerleaders

Super Bowl Championships: None

Nashville, Tennessee

Radio Partner: WKDF 103.3 FM

Hall of Fame Members:
Elvin Bethea
George Blanda
Earl Campbell
Dave Casper
Sid Gillman
Ken Houston
John Henry Johnson
Charlie Joiner
Warren Moon
Mike Munchak

Tailgating takes place in stadium lots. RV parking for season ticket holders; no overnight parking. No saving spaces, rowdy behavior, running, or jogging. Tailgate in front of or behind vehicle only and stay in your space. Need permits for tents or canopies. Coal bins available for charcoal ashes. You can't tailgate downtown, but you can park there and take the pedestrian bridge across the river.

Shuttle info: Nashville MTA's End Zone Express runs from Greer Stadium located at 534 Chestnut Street, and state employee parking lots located at 4th Avenue North and Harrison Street. Services begin 1 1/2 hours before kickoff, ending service 30 minutes after game's end. Buses run on limited basis during game. Cost is $6 round trip.

Washington Redskins

Franchise Colors: Burgundy, Gold, White

Stadium: FedEx Field

Capacity: 86,484

Surface: Grass

Opened: 1997

Phone: (301) 276-6000

Mascot Name: None

Cheerleading Squad Name: Washington Redskins Cheerleaders

Super Bowl Championships: (3)–XVII, XXII, XXVI

Washington, DC

Radio Partner: WJFK 106.7 FM

Tailgating permitted in all stadium lots. Tailgate in front of or behind vehicle only. No buying extra spaces. Put out all flames and grills before game. Ash Dumpsters available. Stadium is 5 minutes from DC.

Shuttle info: Shuttle service provided from cash lots to FedEx Field. Service free for those in cash lot, $5 for anyone in non-Redskin lot. Metro Buses service stadium every 15 minutes. Service begins 2 hours before game, ends 2 hours after game's end. For Monday night games, shuttle service runs from 5 p.m. until 1 a.m. Round trip bus fare costs $5, however, price subject to change without notice.

Hall of Fame Members:
George Allen
Cliff Battles
Sammy Baugh
Bill Dudley
Albert Glen (Turk) Edwards
Ray Flaherty
Joe Gibbs
Ken Houston
Sam Huff
David (Deacon) Jones
Stan Jones
Sonny Jurgensen
Paul Krause
Earl (Curly) Lambeau
Vince Lombardi
George Preston Marshall
Wayne Millner
Bobby Mitchell
John Riggins
Charley Taylor

Boston College Eagles

School Colors: Maroon and Gold

Stadium: Alumni

Capacity: 44,500

Surface: Turf

Opened: 1957

Phone: (617) 552-2886

Mascot Names: Baldwin and Baldwin Jr.

National Championships: None

Heisman Winners: (1) Doug Flutie (1984)

Chestnut Hill, Massachusetts

Radio Partner: WZBC 90.3 FM

> **College Hall of Fame Members:**
> Chet "The Gentle Giant" Gladchuk
> Gene Goodreault
> Mike Holovak
> George "Righteous Reject" Kerr
> Charlie "Chuckin' Charlie" O'Rourke

On-campus parking and tailgating reserved for donors. Only propane grills allowed; no tents, RVs, limos, or other oversized vehicles. No tailgating during game. Lots close at different times depending on game schedule. Nondonors park off campus free at Needham Satellite lot. No tailgating in these lots, no RVs, no overnight parking. Nondonor fans should visit free Fanfest in Flynn Recreation Complex for food and beverages, games, and appearances by mascot, cheerleaders, and band.

Shuttle info: Shuttles run to and from Needham Satellite lot to stadium on a continual basis before, during, and after the game. Service begins 2 hours before game and runs until 2 hours postgame. Buses leave at 10-minute intervals and drop off and pick up in front of the Merkert Chemistry Center on the Beacon Street side of Alumni Stadium.

Top 5 College Football Tailgating Stadiums

There's something special about tailgating at college games. The combination of the students and alumni, the school and team histories, and the way communities wrap their arms around their schools makes for a great tailgating atmosphere. For some schools, every week is a huge celebration. At others, there are rivalry games that have the fans cranking it up a notch. A mix of both is on my list.

1. Ole Miss

Sure they tailgate at other schools, but not like this. When stepping onto the 10 acres of oak tree–shaded grass in the middle of campus known as The Grove, you can be forgiven if you think you've walked into a charity fundraiser. Men in jackets and ties; women in dresses; tables set with china, silver, and centerpieces; cocktails and appetizers served before entrées. This is more than a tailgate party: it's a cocktail and dinner party. It's also a reunion for scores of fans who have attended Ole Miss and tailgated at The Grove for generations. That's why *Sports Illustrated* has named Ole Miss the nation's top tailgating school and the *Sporting News* has called The Grove "the Holy Grail of tailgating sites."

2. Tennessee

Tailgating at Tennessee is just this side of religion for Vols fans. Somewhere around 130,000 people dressed in orange hit Knoxville on game day by air, land, and sea–okay, by water. The Vol Navy is an armada several hundred strong that docks along the Tennessee River to "sterngate" before heading into the stadium. While 104,079 fans take their seats inside the stadium, the rest continue the party outside.

3. LSU

On game day there are about 20,000 fans who show up just to tailgate. (Another 90,000 come to tailgate and go to the game.) The passion of the fans along with the caldrons of gumbo, crawfish etouffee, jambalaya, and other Cajun and Creole specialties help make this a one-of-a-kind tailgate experience. Heck, this is the place where the fans roared so loud after beating Auburn in 1988 it convinced a seismograph there'd been an earthquake.

4. Penn State

A recent winner of *Sports Illustrated's* top tailgate contest, Happy Valley is filled with fans who start arriving days before the game. And while Nittany Lion fans are passionate, it's still a very friendly tailgate atmosphere for visiting fans. I guess that's one reason they call the area Happy Valley. And there must be something to it; in the 1980s *Psychology Today* named State College one of the least stressful places in America.

5. Georgia vs. Florida—Jacksonville, FL

I know, it's just one game a season, but it's not called The World's Largest Outdoor Cocktail Party for nothing. About 100,000 fans show up for the festivities—even though only 80,000 of them can fit in the stadium. But that's not the point. And like any good cocktail party, there's plenty of food as many fans set up several days before game time to fire up their grills and their spirits. (One note: I should say this is the game *formerly* known as The World's Largest Outdoor Cocktail Party since both universities have asked that name not be used any more. Officially, it may not be; in reality it will be for years, if not forever.)

Clemson Tigers

RVs can arrive Friday evening, park in YMCA parking lot for $10 per day Friday through Sunday. Tailgating starts at 8 a.m. and ends at 3 p.m. Keep all tailgating gear within 5 feet of your parking space. Note: For children age 3 to 10, Clemson provides GymSitters. Drop kids off 30 minutes before game; pick them up 30 minutes after. Kids get snacks, craft activities, and T-shirt. Cost is $50 per child, and peace of mind.

School Colors: Orange and Purple

Stadium: Memorial

Capacity: 81,474

Surface: Grass

Opened: 1942

Phone: (864) 656-2270, (864) 656-6556 (GymSitters)

Mascot Names: Tiger and Tiger Cub

National Championships: 1981

Heisman Winners: None

Clemson, South Carolina

Radio Partners: WCCP 104.9 FM

> **College Hall of Fame Members:**
> Banks "Bonnie Banks" McFadden
> Terry Kinard

Shuttle info: All parking within easy walking distance. No shuttles needed.

Duke Blue Devils

RVs can arrive 5 p.m. Friday, park in lot adjacent to PG11 for $25 per day. Cars park for $5. Most tailgaters gather at Blue Devil Tailgate Terrace. Tailgating starts as early as 7 a.m. Saturday; goes on till Sunday. Advertising banners not allowed. University offers good security and relaxed attitude.

School Colors: Royal Blue and White
Stadium: Wallace Wade
Capacity: 33,941
Surface: Grass
Opened: 1929
Phone: (919) 684-7275
Mascot Name: The Blue Devil
National Championships: None
Heisman Winners: None
Durham, North Carolina
Radio Partner: WDNC 620 AM

College Hall of Fame Members:
Fred Crawford
Al "De Ro" DeRogatis
Dan "Tiger" Hill
Steve Lach
George "One Play" McAfee
Mike McGee
Ace Parker
Eric "Eric the Red" Tipton

Shuttle info: All parking within walking distance. No shuttles needed.

Florida State Seminoles

Stadium parking reserved for donors. Best bet: park at Tallahassee Civic Center. Overnight parking $35, or $60 for two nights. Arrive here as early as 10 a.m. Friday. Tailgating runs from 7 a.m. Saturday to noon Sunday. No kegs or tent stakes allowed. Shuttle from civic center runs 2 hours before game. Booster Lots A, B, C, D available to public 30 minutes before game for $75, first-come, first-served.

School Colors: Garnet and Gold

Stadium: Doak S. Campbell

Capacity: 82,000

Surface: Grass

Opened: 1950

Phone: (850) 644-3484, (850) 487-1691 (Tallahassee Civic Center)

Symbol Name: Chief Osceola and Renegade

National Championships: (2)–1939, 1999

Heisman Winners: (2)–Charlie Ward (1993), Chris Weinke (2000)

Tallahassee, Florida

Radio Partners: WTNT 94.9 FM, WNLS 1270 AM

> **College Hall of Fame Members:**
> Fred "Freddie B" Biletnikoff
> Ron "Jingle Joints" Sellers

Shuttle info: Shuttles run from Civic Center continuously, beginning 1 1/2 hours before kickoff and shuttle back until 1 hour after game; $3 round trip, under 12 years free.

Georgia Tech Yellow Jackets

RVs arrive 6 p.m. Friday, park along Tech Parkway, $30 for each RV pass. Display parking pass to reach parking area smoothly. Tailgating starts 7 a.m. Saturday, till noon Sunday. No kegs allowed; no tent stakes allowed. No parking on sidewalks, lawns, green space, or landscaped areas. Those who do will be "booted." Shuttles are free.

School Colors: Old Gold, White, Navy Blue

Stadium: Bobby Dodd

Capacity: 55,000

Surface: Grass

Opened: 1913

Phone: (404) 894-9645

Mascot Name: Buzz

National Championships: (1)–1990

Heisman Winners: None

Atlanta, Georgia

Radio Partner: WQXI 790 AM

....
College Hall of Fame Members:
Joe "O-gee-Chideah (Big Brave)"
Guyon
Buck Flowers Davidson
Maxie Baughan
Bobby Davis
Bill Fincher
George Morris
Larry Morris
Peter "Peter The Great" Pund
Everett "Strup" Strupper
Ray Beck
Randy Rhino
....

Shuttle info: Traffic too congested to allow for Tech Trolley or Stinger Bus Services. Atlanta's MARTA bus system available at the North Avenue. Train Station, or the #13 bus line, for $1.75.

Maryland Terrapins

RVs arrive evening before game, park in Lots 4I, 4J, and 4B for $40 for the weekend. University prohibits kegs and grilling inside garages. Alcohol patrols and campus police keep things peaceful. Keep everything orderly and you'll be fine. Tailgaters urged to remove all trash when leaving. Got car or RV trouble? Call (301) 314-4CAR for help with gas, battery problems, lock-outs, etc. Visit Terrapin Tailgate adjacent to Parking Lot 1 and Ludwig Field for official tailgate party.

School Colors: Red, White, Black and Gold
Stadium: Byrd
Capacity: 48,055
Surface: Grass
Opened: 1950
Phone: (301) 314-7275, (301) 314-4CAR (Motorist Assistance Vehicle)
Mascot Name: Testudo
National Championships: (1)–1953
Heisman Winners: None
College Park, Maryland
Radio Partners: WMAL 630 AM, WJFK 1300 AM, WHFS 105.7 FM

College Hall of Fame Members:
Dick "Little Mo" Modzelewski
Jack Scarbath
Bob Ward
Randy "The Manster" White
Bob Pellegrini
Stan Jones

Shuttle info: Quick Bus shuttle service available at College Park Metro Station to Lot Q, near Byrd Stadium. Buses run every 20 minutes starting 3 hours before kickoff. Shuttles return to College Park Metro Station for 1 hour after the game. Quick Bus is also available from Lots 4, 9, and 11 and Mowatt Lane Garage to Lot Q on a more limited schedule.

Miami Hurricanes

Tailgating here can be tricky: restrictions change from game to game. Parking around stadium for donors. Depending on location parking prices range from $7 to $450. Call ahead for details and locations of available satellite lots. Try for a spot in Lot 18 ($7) at NW 12 Street and 13th Avenue. Shuttles available, price varies from $8.75 to free, depending on which you use. Good luck!

School Colors: Orange, Green and White

Stadium: Orange Bowl

Capacity: 72,319

Surface: Grass

Opened: 1935

Phone: (305) 284-6699

> **College Hall of Fame Members:**
> Don "Bull" Bosseler
> Ted "The Mad Stork" Hendricks

Mascot Name: Sebastian the Ibis

National Championships: (5)–1983, 1987, 1989, 1991, 2001

Heisman Winners: (2)–Vinny Testaverde (1986), Gino Torretta (1992)

Coral Gables, Florida

Radio Partners: WQAM 560 AM, WNMA 1020 AM (Spanish)

Shuttle info: City Park & Ride available at Tamiami Park Metrobus terminal (117th Avenue SW and 24th Street, by batting cages) and Golden Glades Interchange, both for $8.75. From Culmer Metrorail station, shuttle is $1.25. Lot 18 has free shuttle service, starting 2 1/2 hours before kickoff, and for 1 hour postgame. Service Park & Ride locations begins 2 hours before kickoff, ends 1 hour postgame.

North Carolina Tar Heels

RVs arrive 5 p.m. Friday and park in the Friday Center Park & Ride lot. Tailgating starts 8 a.m. game day, ends at midnight. Expect to see lots of barbecue, especially Parker's Barbecue. Shuttles are available and free. Alcohol's not allowed—keep it in cups and be discreet. No open flames allowed either. Athletic Department sponsors Tarheel Town with concessions and games for kids. Worth a visit.

School Colors: Carolina Blue & White
Stadium: Kenan Memorial
Capacity: 60,000
Surface: Grass
Opened: 1927
Phone: (919) 962-3951
Mascot Name: Rameses the Ram
National Championships: None
Heisman Winners: None
Chapel Hill, North Carolina
Radio Partner: WCHL 1360 AM

College Hall of Fame Members:
Barney Poole
Charlie "Choo Choo" Justice
Art Weiner
Don McCauley
Hunter Carpenter

Shuttle info: Tarheel Express Service operates from Jones Ferry Road; Friday Center Park & Ride lot next to Continuing Education Center; Southern Village Park & Ride lot, between Culbreth and Dogwood Acres Road; southern end of University Mall at Estes Drive, outside Dillard's store. Round trip is $5. Return trips run for 30 minutes postgame.

North Carolina State Wolfpack

RVs park at North Carolina State Fairgrounds, adjacent to stadium. Fairground has 300 RV sites with hookups, $20 a day. Stay as long as you like. Tailgating starts 4 hours before game, stops at midnight. No kegs; tent stays within your space and must be flame retardant. For medical emergencies, dial 911 and on-site ambulance will respond. Local tailgating treat: whole smoked or barbecued pig.

School Colors: Red and White
Stadium: Carter-Finley
Capacity: 53,800
Surface: Grass
Opened: 1966
Phone: (800) 310-PACK
Mascot Names: Mr. Ruf and Ms. Ruf
National Championships: None
Heisman Winners: None
Raleigh, North Carolina
Radio Partners: WPTF 680 AM

College Hall of Fame Members:
Roman "Gabe" Gabriel
Jack "Spindle Legs" McDowall
Jim Ritcher

Shuttle info: Free Wolfline Bus Route 6 Vet School runs from corner of Gardner and Hillsboro to Stadium every 10 minutes during peak times and every 15 minutes off-peak times, on days that school and exams are in session. Werewolf B Night Service covers this route in the evening. There are no shuttles specifically designated for game days.

Virginia Cavaliers

RVs park at University Hall parking lot, and approved grassy areas. RV spots open at 8 a.m. game day, first-come, first-served, and free. Tailgating runs from 8 a.m. 'til midnight. Parking garages are available, but not for tailgating. Numerous private lots around town. Those in university lots must use gas grills, not charcoal. Leave tents at home; take trash with you.

School Colors: Orange and Blue
Stadium: Scott
Capacity: 61,500
Surface: Grass
Opened: 1931
Phone: (800) 542-UVA1
Mascot Name: The Cavalier
National Championships: None
Heisman Winners: None
Charlottesville, Virginia
Radio Partner: WRVA 1140 AM

College Hall of Fame Members:
Bill "Bullet Bill" Dudley
Tom Scott
Joe Palumbo

Shuttle info: All parking within walking distance. No shuttles needed.

Virginia Tech Hokies

Visiting RVs park in Lot 17 (Duckpond overflow lot) for $15, first-come, first-served. Those with season passes park in Lot 3 or Lot 16. RVs arrive 6 p.m. Friday. Tailgating starts 7 a.m. game day, till midnight. Tents not allowed; tailgaters limited to one space. Alcohol permitted only in donor lots. This rule isn't strictly enforced, as long as you're discreet. Most people park in different lots throughout town—shuttles available.

School Colors: Burnt Orange and Maroon
Stadium: Lane
Capacity: 66,230
Surface: Grass
Opened: 1965
Phone: (540) 231-3200, (540) 231-6618 (RV Parking Information)
Mascot Name: Hokie Bird
National Championships: None
Heisman Winners: None
Blacksburg, Virginia
Radio Partner: WBRW 105.3 FM

College Hall of Fame Members:
Carroll Dale
Frank Loria
Hunter Carpenter

Shuttle info: Blacksburg Transit provides a free shuttle service from satellite parking lots at Blacksburg High School and New Blacksburg Middle School to the stadium.

Wake Forest Demon Deacons

RVs arrive 5 p.m. Fridays, park at LJVM Coliseum Lot for $8, same as cars. Additional RV parking with hookups at city-run campground. No charcoal grills, glass containers, or hard liquor. No gas powered generators or external stereo systems allowed. No tailgating during the game. Keep tents in grassy areas.

School Colors: Old Gold and Black
Stadium: Groves
Capacity: 31,500
Surface: Grass
Opened: 1935, 1968
Phone: (336) 758-5753
Mascot Name: The Deacon
National Championships: None
Heisman Winners: None
College Hall of Fame Members: None
Winston-Salem, North Carolina
Radio Partner: WBRF 98.1 FM

Shuttle info: All parking within walking distance. No shuttles needed.

Baylor Bears

Visiting RVs can't park on campus. Go to I-35 RV Park & Resort for $21–$24 a day, follow their rules. Cars can park on campus, $10 per game. Visitors can also picnic at Creekside Tailgate area (no vehicles here). Tailgating starts 8 a.m., stops at beginning of game. University has chairs, tables, grills to rent if needed. No alcohol allowed on campus. Heavy police presence deals swiftly with public drunk-and-disorderly fans.

School Colors: Green and Gold
Stadium: Floyd Casey
Capacity: 50,000
Surface: Grass
Opened: 1935
Phone: (254) 710-3804, (254) 829-0698 (I-35 RV Park & Resort)
Mascot Name: Bruiser
National Championships: None
Heisman Winners: None
Waco, Texas
Radio Partner: KRZI 1660 AM

College Hall of Fame Members:
Larry Elkins
Bill Glass
Barton Koch
Mike Singletary
Jim Ray Smith

Shuttle info: Shuttles run from Bill Daniel Student Center to Touchdown Alley starting 2 hours prior to kick-off. No shuttles available for nonstudent fans.

Colorado Buffaloes

Parking and tailgating lots open 10:30 a.m. game day. RVs and oversized vehicles park in Lot 470; pay $20 per spaces needed (RVs need 3, cars need 1, limos 2). There is no overnight parking. Tailgating can continue throughout game. Open containers only allowed inside tailgating areas.

School Colors: Silver, Gold, and Black
Stadium: Folsom Field
Capacity: 53,750
Surface: Turf
Opened: 1924
Phone: (303) 492-7384
Mascot Name: Chip
National Championships: (1)–1990
Heisman Winners: (1)–Rashaan Salaam (1994)
Boulder, Colorado
Radio Partner: KOA 850 AM

> **College Hall of Fame Members:**
> Dick Anderson
> Joe Romig
> Byron "Whizzer" White

Shuttle info: All parking and tailgating within easy walking distance. No shuttles needed.

Iowa State Cyclones

RVs can arrive Friday before game, 5 p.m. in Lots G2 and G3 for $30, or Lot 93 for $20. Cars pay $8 to $10 depending on location. Tailgating starts 6 hours prior to game and goes until noon Sunday, when everyone leaves. No glass bottles allowed; leave kegs, funnels, and beer balls at home. Canopies must be no larger than 10 x 10 feet.

School Colors: Cardinal and Gold
Stadium: Jack Trice Field
Capacity: 45,814
Surface: Grass
Opened: 1975
Phone: (515) 294-3388
Mascot Name: Cy
National Championships: None
Heisman Winners: None
Ames, Iowa
Radio Partners: KASI 1430 AM, KCCQ 105.1 FM

College Hall of Fame Members:
Ed Bock

Shuttle info: Free shuttles provided throughout parking areas to stadium complex. Shuttles start 3 hours prior to kickoff, ends 1 hour after game's conclusion.

Kansas Jayhawks

Visitors park for free at Lot 72 or Lot 90, starting Friday at 5 p.m. Tailgating may start upon arrival, and ends 2 hours after game time. RVs may stay until Sunday afternoon. Other lots carry a charge of $10. Kegs, beer balls, etc, are forbidden.

School Colors: Crimson and Blue
Stadium: Memorial
Capacity: 50,250
Surface: Turf
Opened: 1921
Phone: (785) 864-7275
Mascot Name: Big Jay
National Championships: None
Heisman Winners: None
Lawrence, Kansas
Radio Partners: KLWN 1320 AM, KLZR 105.9 FM

> **College Hall of Fame Members:**
> Ray Evans
> John Hadl
> Gale Sayers

Shuttle info: Catch a ride at Irving Hill Rd, just north of Burge Union or the parking lot south of Robinson Center. One way is $2, round trip $3 per person. Shuttle starts 2 hours before kickoff.

Kansas State Wildcats

Reserved RV spots in East and West stadium lots; only Booster Club members can stay overnight before or after. General parking for all vehicles in Lot 9, Chester Peters Recreation Center lot, or satellite lots surrounding the stadium and other paved campus lots. General parking is $25 for RVs, $10 for cars. No alcohol allowed on campus; no ground fires; no bikes, skateboards, or scooters in parking lots.

School Colors: Purple and White
Stadium: Billy Snyder Family Football
Capacity: 50,000
Surface: Turf
Opened: 1968
Phone: (800) 221-2287
Mascot Name: Willie Wildcat
National Championships: None
Heisman Winners: None
Manhattan, Kansas
Radio Partners: KMAN 1350 AM, KMKF 101.5 FM

College Hall of Fame Members:
Gary Spani

Shuttle info: All parking and tailgating within easy walking distance. No shuttles needed.

Missouri Tigers

RVs park at the Hearnes Center, $50 for weekend. Cars park for $10 in various garages, parking lots, and streets. Tailgaters must stay within their space. No kegs, beer balls, or bulk quantities of alcohol allowed on campus or campus parking areas. Dispose of used coals in specially marked barrels. Note: Childcare available at Pigskin Preschool, located in Child Development Lab at Stanley Hall (nationally recognized childcare facility). Preschool opens 2 hours before game, closes 2 hours after game's end. Children from 6 weeks to 10 years welcome. First child $40, additional siblings $25 each.

School Colors: Black and Gold

Stadium: Memorial

Capacity: 68,349

Surface: Turf

Opened: 1926

Phone: (573) 882-7201 or (800) CAT-PAWS

Mascot Name: Truman the Tiger

National Championships: None

Heisman Winners: None

Columbia, Missouri

Radio Partners: KFRU 1400 AM, KBXR 102.3 FM

College Hall of Fame Members:
Paul Christman
Darold Jenkins
Johnny Roland
Bob Steuber
Ed "Brick" Travis
Roger Wehrli
Kellen Winslow

Shuttle info: Courtesy shuttle available from south field level (adjacent to Lot G) to the East and West Gates. Shuttle starts 1 1/2 hours before game, during halftime, and runs until 1 hour after game.

Nebraska Cornhuskers

No RVs on campus, unless members of Booster's clubs. Most campus parking reserved. City offers numerous parking garages with prepaid, reserved spots for $6–$11. Best bet for tailgaters are lots near state fairgrounds on north side of campus for $5–$10. Largest unreserved campus lots located at Bio Science Greenhouses, between Vine and R Streets. RVers should park rigs in nearby RV parks: Lancaster Event Center, Lincoln's Camp-A-Way, and State Fairgrounds. When tailgating, remember Lincoln's open container laws and other city ordinances. Note: Childcare available for kids 2–12 years old at Jr. Blackshirts Day Camp, in Campus Recreation Center. Camp opens 90 minutes before game, closes 45 minutes after game's end. You MUST preregister for camp; $20 per child.

School Colors: Scarlet and Cream

Stadium: Memorial

Capacity: 73,918

Surface: Turf

Opened: 1923

Phone: (402) 472-1800

Mascot Name: Herbie Husker

National Championships: (5) *1970, 1971, 1994, 1995, *1997

Heisman Winners: (3)–Johnny Rodgers (1972), Mike Rozier (1983), Eric Crouch (2001)

Lincoln, Nebraska

Radio Partners: KLIN 1400 AM, KFAB 1110 AM

College Hall of Fame Members:
Bob "The Boomer" Brown
Guy Chamberlin
Sam Francis
Rich Glover
Wayne Meylan
Dave Rimington
Bobby Reynolds
Johnny Rodgers
George Sauer
Clarence Swanson
Ed Weir

Shuttle info: Big Red Express service stops at seven locations around town, $8 round trip. You'll need exact change.

Oklahoma Sooners

Visiting RVs park at Lloyd Noble Center. The Center has 130 spaces with hookups at $80 per weekend, 88 spaces without hookups at $30 per weekend. RVs start arriving as early as 5 p.m. Friday. Tailgating starts 7 a.m. game day, running until kickoff. No tailgating during the game. Open container policy strictly enforced. No pets allowed.

School Colors: Crimson and Cream
Stadium: Gaylord Family-Oklahoma Memorial
Capacity: 82,112
Surface: Grass
Opened: 1924
Phone: (405) 325-4666
Mascot Name: Sooner Schooner
National Championships: (7)–1950, 1955, 1956, *1974, 1975, 1985, 2000
Heisman Winners: (4)–Billy Vessels (1952), Steve Owens (1969), Billy Sims (1978), Jason White (2003)
Norman, Oklahoma
Radio Partners: KOKC 1520 AM, KRXO 107.7 FM

Shuttle info: Shuttle runs from Lloyd Noble Center to Stadium, $2.

College Hall of Fame Members:
Kurt Burris
Tony Casillas
Forest Geyer
Keith Jackson
Tommy "Shoo-Fly" McDonald
Jim Owens
Steve Owens
Greg Pruitt
Claude Reeds
J. D. Roberts
Lee Roy Selmon
Billy Sims
Jerry Tubbs
Billy "Curly" Vessels
Joe Washington
Jim Weatherall
Waddy Young

Oklahoma State Cowboys

Visiting RVs park for free in Lot 81 on Hall of Fame Ave, east of the Physical Plant. Lot opens at 10:30 a.m. Tailgating runs from 10:30 a.m. until midnight including during game. No overnight parking. Leave pets at home, take garbage with you. Note: Childcare available at Stillwater YMCA for kids 3 and up, starting 1 hour before game and ending 1 hour after game's end.

School Colors: Orange and Black
Stadium: Boone-Pickens
Capacity: 82,112
Surface: Turf
Opened: 1920
Phone: (405) 744-5000
Mascot Name: Pistol Pete
National Championships: None
Heisman Winners: (1)–Barry Sanders (1988)
Stillwater, Oklahoma
Radio Partner: KSPI 93.7 FM

> **College Hall of Fame Members:**
> Bob Fenimore
> Barry Sanders

Shuttle info: Shuttle service provided to POSSE (season ticket holder/donor) parking lots.

Texas Longhorns

Non-Longhorn Foundation RV parking available in Lot 115 on a space available basis. Check-in begins at 3 p.m. Thursday before home games. Fee is $350 per game. Cars park for $5 to $10 depending on lot. Tailgating runs 5 p.m. Friday, until 2 hours after game's end. No open flames allowed in parking garages. Be mindful of local open container laws.

School Colors: Burnt Orange and White
Stadium: Royal-Memorial
Capacity: 80,082
Surface: Grass
Opened: 1924
Phone: (512) 478-1833
Mascot Name: Bevo
National Championships: (4)–1963, 1969, *1970, 2005
Heisman Winners: (2)–Earl Campbell (1972), Ricky Williams (1998)
Austin, Texas
Radio Partner: KVET 98.1 FM

Shuttle info: Capital Metro provides shuttle service $5 round trip. Pickup locations are UT Intramural Fields parking lots at 51st and Guadalupe Street, and northwest side of Barton Creek Mall.

College Hall of Fame Members:
Earl Campbell
Chris Gilbert
Malcolm "Mal" Kutner
Bobby "Gadabout Gladiator" Layne
Roosevelt Leaks
Bud McFadin
Tommy Nobis
James "Rabbit" Saxton Jr.
Harley Sewell
Jerry Sisemore
Bud Sprague
Harrison Stafford

Texas A&M Aggies

Visiting RVs park in Lot 100E, at $60 for the weekend, by online reservation only. Visitors can arrive as early as 3 p.m. Friday, stay until 2 p.m. Sunday. Tailgating starts 5 hours prior to kickoff, continues through game until 2 p.m. Sunday. Post Oak Mall has free parking with shuttle service. No tailgating in parking garages. No parking in grass or lawns; no parking in streets or bike lanes.

School Colors: Maroon and White

Stadium: Kyle Field

Capacity: 82,600

Surface: Grass

Opened: 1925

Phone: (979) 862-2551

Mascot Name: Reveille VII

National Championships: (1)–1939

Heisman Winners: (1)–John David Crow (1957)

College Station, Texas

Radio Partners: WTAW 1620 AM

Shuttle info: Free shuttle from Post Oak Mall lots runs 3 hours prior to kickoff until 2 hours after game.

College Hall of Fame Members:
John David Crow
Dave Elmendorf
Joel Hunt
John Kimbrough
Charlie Krueger
Jack "Gabby" Pardee
Joe Routt
Joe Utay

Texas Tech Red Raiders

Visiting RVs can park in United Spirit Arena as early as 5:30 Friday at no charge. All must depart by Sunday morning. Tailgating starts upon arrival and runs until departure. Keep all gear within parking space; don't block traffic.

School Colors: Scarlet and Black
Stadium: Jones AT&T
Capacity: 53,702
Surface: Turf
Opened: 1947
Phone: (806) 742-3811
Mascot Name: Raider Red
National Championships: None
Heisman Winners: None
Lubbock, Texas
Radio Partner: KKAM 1340 AM

College Hall of Fame Members:
Donny "The Golden Palomino" Anderson
Hub Bechtol
E. J. Holub

Shuttle info: Citibus provides shuttle from United Spirit Arena, $5 per person.

Cincinnati Bearcats

Two lots for RVs, first-come, first served, $21. All parking within walking distance. Tailgating may continue through game. Keep alcohol in cups; be mindful of open container laws. You must have a fire extinguisher. No alcohol or grills in parking garages. Check out BearCats Kids Zone and Cattitude at Varsity Village, both are family friendly activities starting 2 1/2 hours before game.

School Colors: Red and Black
Stadium: Nippert
Capacity: 35,000
Surface: Turf
Opened: 1924
Phone: (513) 556-2287
Mascot Name: Bearcat
National Championships: None
Heisman Winners: None
College Hall of Fame Members: None
Cincinnati, Ohio
Radio Partner: WLW 700 AM

Shuttle info: Check out the Golf Cart Ambassadors, located near high traffic areas and garages starting 2 hours before, and 30 minutes after, the game.

Connecticut Huskies

Gates open 8 a.m. game day for all vehicles. RVs park in designated areas only. No kegs and no drinking games; no charcoal or oversized grills; no glass containers; no blocking traffic or tossing footballs or Frisbees. No tailgating during the game. Keep coolers and grills in front of or behind vehicles.

School Colors: Blue and White
Stadium: Rentschler Field
Capacity: 40,000
Surface: Grass
Opened: 2003
Phone: (877) 288-2666
Mascot Name: Jonathan XII
National Championships: None
Heisman Winners: None
College Hall of Fame Members: None
Storrs, Connecticut
Radio Partner: WHUS 91.7 FM

Shuttle info: All parking within walking distance, shuttles not needed.

Louisville Cardinals

Save a buck and park at the Fairgrounds for $5. A bit of a hike to the stadium, though. RVs park at surface lots west of stadium, and at Kentucky Fair & Expo Center. Plastic cups preferred; no glass or open containers.

School Colors: Red and Black
Stadium: Papa John's Cardinal
Capacity: 42,000
Surface: Grass
Opened: 1998
Phone: (502) 852-5863
Mascot Name: Cardinal Bird
National Championships: None
Heisman Winners: None
College Hall of Fame Members: None
Louisville, Kentucky
Radio Partner: WHAS 840 AM

Shuttle info: There are golf carts available for people who need help getting to the stadium. Public bus routes drop off in the bus lane adjacent to Floyd Street.

Pittsburgh Panthers

RVs aren't allowed. All campus lots presold by season. Use the Park & Ride lots downtown. Keep alcohol in cups; no glass or open containers and no kegs. No charcoal, or oversized grills; no open flame fires. No tailgating during game. LAZ parking representatives on-site for assistance.

School Colors: Blue and Gold
Stadium: Heinz Field
Capacity: 64,450
Surface: Grass
Opened: 1994
Phone: (412) 648-8200
Mascot Name: "ROC" the Panther
National Championships: (2)–1937, 1976
Heisman Winners: (1)–Tony Dorsett (1976)
Pittsburgh, Pennsylvania
Radio Partner: WTAW 1250 AM

Shuttle info: Multiple Park & Ride lots downtown offer shuttle service, only $1.25 each way. Downtown shuttle service to Heinz Field is available on the 98B Smithfield Street Bridge and 98D Strip District routes, while North Side service is offered from the 14S Beaver Avenue Park & Ride lot.

> **College Hall of Fame Members:**
> Joe Thompson Geneva
> Ave "Li'l Abner" Daniell
> Tom Davies
> Mike Ditka
> Joe Donchess
> Tony Dorsett
> Marshall "Biggie" Goldberg
> George "Tank" McLaren
> Bob Peck
> Joe "Mugsy" Skladany
> Herb Stein
> Hube Wagner
> Hugh Green
> Bill Fralic
> Joe Schmidt
> Dan Marino
> Jim "Jimbo" Covert
> Mark May

Rutgers Scarlet Knights

Parking lots open 3 hours before kickoff; only 15-minute walk to stadium. No kegs, no open fires of any kind, no glass. But you can tailgate during the game. Receive special discounts from downtown merchants with game ticket before and after game.

School Colors: Scarlet and White

Stadium: Rutgers

Capacity: 41,500

Surface: Turf

Opened: 1994

Phone: (732) 445-2766 (Ticket Office), (732) 445-4223 (Facilities)

Mascot Name: The Scarlet Knight

National Championships: None

Heisman Winners: None

New Brunswick/Piscataway, New Jersey

Radio Partner: WOR 710 AM

> **College Hall of Fame Members:**
> Homer "Pop" Hazel
> Paul "Robey" Robeson
> Alex Kroll

Shuttle info: New Brunswick Parking Authority's free shuttle bus to and from the stadium. Free Shuttle Buses beginning 3 hours prior to kickoff just outside the Rutgers Bookstore on Albany Street; they return you to Ferren Deck after game.

South Florida Bulls

RVs pay $5 per space (about $15 to $20). Five lots available for single-game parking: Lot 6, Lot 22A, Lot 22D, Lot 22E, Lot 22F. USF now has 4,000 parking spaces within 1,000 yards of stadium. No overnight parking.

School Colors: Green and Gold
Stadium: Raymond James
Capacity: 65,657
Surface: Grass
Opened: 1988
Phone: (800) 462-8557
Mascot Name: Rocky the Bull
National Championships: None
Heisman Winners: None
College Hall of Fame Members: None
Tampa, Florida
Radio Partners: WDAE 620 AM, WFLA 970 AM

Shuttle info: Bull Runner Shuttle available from Park & Ride Lots 18A and 18B; cost included in parking fee.

Syracuse Orange

RVs can arrive as early as 6 p.m. day before game and overnight at Skytop Road lot. Call parking number to reserve space. You can tailgate during game. Be extra careful with grills. If you're an out-of-towner, be sure to try Hoffman hotdogs and salt potatoes—they're dee-licious.

School Colors: Orange and Blue
Stadium: Carrier Dome
Capacity: 49,262
Surface: Turf
Opened: 1980
Phone: (315) 443-2121 (Ticket Office), (315) 443-4652 (Parking)
Mascot Name: Otto the Orange
National Championships: (1)–1959
Heisman Winners: (1)–Ernie Davis (1961)
Syracuse, New York
Radio Partners: WAER 88.3 FM, WJZP 89.1 FM, WNSS 1260 AM

Shuttle info: Shuttle bus service to and from Skytop to the Carrier Dome (College Place drop-off and pickup) is included in the parking fee.

College Hall of Fame Members:
Joe "Doc" Alexander
Larry "Zonk" Csonka
Ernie "The Elmira Express" Davis
Vic Hanson
Floyd Little
Jim "First Down" Brown
Tim Green

West Virginia Mountaineers

Lots open for RVs 6 p.m. Friday before the game. Best bet: single-game RVs and cars should use free parking at WVU Coliseum and designated areas on the Evansdale campus. You must call ahead for RV permit. Cars have separate permit. Permits are not interchangeable. Tents are limited to 12 x 12 feet. Leave kegs and artificial noisemakers at home.

School Colors: Old Gold and Blue
Stadium: Milan Puskar
Capacity: 63,500
Surface: Turf
Opened: 1980
Phone: (304) 293-3541 (Ticket Office), (304) 293-5621 (Athletic Director)
Mascot Name: The Mountaineer
National Championships: None
Heisman Winners: None
Morgantown, West Virginia
Radio Partners: WAJR 1440 AM, WWVU 91.7 FM

College Hall of Fame Members:
Bruce Bosley
Sam Huff
Ira "Rat" Rodgers
Joe "Jumbo Joe" Stydahar

Shuttle info: Shuttle service to the stadium available for $3.50 round trip.

Illinois Fighting Illini

RVs and tailgaters arrive early as 7 a.m. RVs park in Lot A, $35; cars are $15. Visitors should arrive at stadium from south or east for easier parking. No balloons or banners with ads; no open fires, no political campaigning. Tents must be 10 x 10 feet or smaller.

School Colors: Orange and Blue
Stadium: Memorial
Capacity: 69,249
Surface: Turf
Opened: 1923
Phone: (866) ILLINI-1
Mascot Name: None
National Championships: (4)–1914, 1919, 1923, 1927
Heisman Winners: None
Urbana-Champaign, Illinois
Radio Partners: WDWS 1400 AM, WHMS 97.5 FM

Shuttle info: All parking within walking distance, no shuttles needed.

College Hall of Fame Members:
Dick Butkus
Al Brosky
Chuck Carney
J.C. "Mr. Zoom" Caroline
Jim Grabowski
Red "The Galloping Ghost" Grange
Bart Macomber
Bernie Shively
David Williams
Buddy Young

Indiana Hoosiers

RVs arrive 6 p.m. Friday, park at Gate 11 for $40. All parking within easy walking distance; no shuttles needed. Tailgating starts 7 a.m. Saturday. No tailgating during game, but tailgating may resume after game's end (enforced by university police.) Lawn furniture's permitted, but not "indoor" furniture. Canopies are allowed but mustn't impede traffic. No tents, or glass containers allowed. Overnight tailgaters should leave Sunday morning.

School Colors: Cream and Crimson

Stadium: Memorial

Capacity: 52,355

Surface: Turf

Opened: 1960

Phone: (812) 855-0847

Mascot Name: Hoosier

National Championships: None

Heisman Winners: None

Bloomington, Indiana

Radio Partner: WHCC 105.1 FM

College Hall of Fame Members:
Zora Clevenger
Pete "Big Dog" Pihos
George Taliaferro
John Tavener

Shuttle info: All parking within walking distance, no shuttles needed.

Iowa Hawkeyes

RVs arrive 6 p.m. Friday, park in Lots 43, 1F & 2F for $20 per day; cars pay $10. Free parking, shuttle service available from Hancher Commuter Lot and Hawkeye Commuter Lot, 2 hours prior to kick off. Public parking for RVs available at Finkbine Golf Course and commuter lots. Tailgating may continue during game–just keep it within your space, leave glass containers home.

School Colors: Black and Old Gold
Stadium: Kinnick
Capacity: 70,397
Surface: Grass
Opened: 1929
Phone: (319) 335-9431
Mascot Name: Herky the Hawkeye
National Championships: (1) *1958
Heisman Winners: Nile Kinnick (1939)
Iowa City, Iowa
Radio Partner: KXIC 800 AM

College Hall of Fame Members:
Aubrey Devine
Randy Duncan
Calvin Jones
Alex "Mad Duck" Karras
Nile Kinnick
Gordon Locke
Duke Slater

Shuttle info: Hawkeye Express Train transports fans 3 hours prior to kickoff, resuming at start of fourth quarter. To ride, park south of U.S. Highway 6, south of Coral Ridge Mall. Round-trip $10 per person, children 12 and under free. Lots O and P have free shuttle service.

Michigan Wolverines

RVs park in Pioneer High School's Purple Lot, $150 for weekend. Season Reserved RV pass holders can park 5 p.m. Friday; non-reserved RVs park Saturday 6 a.m., $125 for weekend. More RV parking at Varsity Tennis Center in Brown Lot, Friday arrivals $80 per weekend, Saturday (8 a.m.) arrivals $30; both stay 'til Sunday. Cars park in Brown Lot, Driving Range lot, both $15. Shuttles available, $4 round-trip. Tailgating starts 8 a.m. Saturday, continues through game. No alcohol in Pioneer High School lot.

School Colors: Maize and Blue

Stadium: Michigan

Capacity: 107,501

Surface: GrassTurf

Opened: 1927

Phone: (734) 647-9977, (734) 994-2330 (Pioneer High School)

Mascot Name: Wolverine

National Championships: (11)–*1901, *1902, *1903, *1904, *1918, *1923, 1932, *1933, *1947, 1948, *1997

Heisman Winners: (3)–Tom Harmon (1940), Desmond Howard (1991), Charles Woodson (1997)

Ann Arbor, Michigan

Radio Partners: WTKA 1050 AM, CKLW 800 AM, WOMC 104.3 FM

Shuttle info: Ann Arbor Transit Authority (AATA) offers The Football Ride between Michigan Stadium and Ann Arbor hotels and motels, UM parking areas, the Michigan Union, and downtown. It costs $2 one way, $4 round trip per person. It runs every 20 minutes, starting 2 hours before kickoff, dropping off fans at Gate 2. Shuttles run for 1 hour post-game. During rain or heavy snow, the shuttle runs throughout the game.

College Hall of Fame Members:

Albert Benbrook

Anthony Carter

Bob Chappuis

Tom Curtis

Dan Dierdorf

Pete Elliott

Benny Friedman

Tom "Old 98" Harmon

Ron Johnson

Harry Kipke

Ron Kramer

Jim Mandich

Reggie McKenzie

Harry Newman

Bennie Oosterbaan

Merv Pregulman

Germany Schulz

Neil Snow

Ernie Vick

Bob Westfall

Albert "Ox" Wistert

Francis "Whitey" Wistert

Michigan State Spartans

RVs park in lots across from the Grounds Department and in Physical Plant Parking Lot, for $30. No overnight parking. Tailgating starts 7 a.m., 9 a.m., or 1 p.m. depending on time of game. Lawn, outdoor furniture only. No kegs or beer balls. No drinking game gear. No trailers, including pig roasters. Oversized trucks park in RV parking. Dispose of all trash properly. No canopies over 10 x 10 feet. Munn Field available for alcohol-free tailgating.

School Colors: Green and White

Stadium: Spartan

Capacity: 72,027

Surface: Grass

Opened: 1957

Phone: (517) 355-8440

Mascot Name: Sparty

National Championships: (3)–*1952, *1965, *1966

Heisman Winners: None

East Lansing, Michigan

Radio Partners: WJIM 1240 AM, WMMQ 94.9 FM

Shuttle info: Green Line available at Lot 89, $3 round-trip.

College Hall of Fame Members:
Don Coleman
John Pingel
Bubba Smith
Brad Van Pelt
George Webster

Minnesota Golden Gophers

RVs and tailgaters park in UM Tailgating Lot, at Rapid Park, $12 per space used. Lot opens 4 hours before kickoff. No overnight parking. Free shuttle service provided. Not many restrictions—just bring lots of trash bags. Receptacles provided, and university will pick up bagged trash left behind.

School Colors: Maroon and Gold

Stadium: Hubert H. Humphrey Metrodome

Capacity: 64,172

Surface: Turf

Opened: 1982

Phone: (612) 332-4735

Mascot Name: Goldy the Gopher

National Championships: (6)–1934, *1935, 1936, 1940, 1941, *1960

Heisman Winners: (1)–Bruce Smith (1941)

Minneapolis, Minnesota

Radio Partners: WCCO 830 AM, KBEM 88.5 FM

College Hall of Fame Members:
Bert Baston
Bobby Bell
Tom Brown
George Franck
Paul Giel
Herb Joesting
Pug Lund
Bobby "Rube" Marshall
John McGovern
Bronko Nagurski
Leo "The Lion" Nomellini
Bruce "Boo" Smith
Clayton Tonnemaker
Ed Widseth
Dick Wildung

Shuttle info: Extensive, free shuttle service available, with 5 campus stops. Metrodome Shuttle Bus Service starts 1½ hours before kickoff, with service every 5–7 minutes. The return shuttle runs until 45 minutes after game's end.

Northwestern Wildcats

Overnight RV parking available at Campus Lot 2, $30 a day. RVs can arrive 6 p.m. Friday. No parking available around Ryan Field, make use of numerous city and campus lots. Tailgating starts 7 a.m. Saturday, and continues throughout game. Only real restriction is no glass containers. Otherwise, use common sense. RVs leave by 12 noon Sunday.

School Colors: Purple and White
Stadium: Ryan Field
Capacity: 47,130
Surface: Grass
Opened: 1926
Phone: (847) 491-CATS
Mascot Name: Willie the Wildcat
National Championships: None
Heisman Winners: None
College Hall of Fame Members: None
Evanston, Illinois
Radio Partner: WGN 720 AM

Shuttle info: Free shuttle service provided for anyone parking in an on-campus lot, starting 2 hours before game, running until 1 hour post-game.

The Ohio State Buckeyes

Football parking varies, depending on which game and whether other varsity sports (basketball) are also playing. In general, RVs arrive Friday before game, sometimes early as 7 a.m., and park in Buckeye Lots across from Jesse Owens Memorial Stadium. RV is parking first-come, first-served, $30 to $50 for weekend, depending on game. Cars park for $10. Open container laws in effect; be discreet. Grills only allowed on surfaced lots.

School Colors: Scarlet and Gray
Stadium: Ohio
Capacity: 101,568
Surface: Grass
Opened: 1922
Phone: (614) 292-2624
Mascot Name: Brutus Buckeye
National Championships: (7)–1942, *1954, *1957, *1961, 1968, *1970, 2002
Heisman Winners: (7)–Les Horvath (1944), Vic Janowicz (1950), Howard Cassady (1955), Archie Griffin (1974, 1975), Eddie George (1995), Troy Smith (2006)
Columbus, Ohio
Radio Partners: WBNS 1460 AM & 97.1 FM

Shuttle info: Free shuttle service for fans parked on West Campus.

College Hall of Fame Members:
Warren Amling
Hopalong Cassady
Jim "Big Jim" Daniell
Bob Ferguson
Wes Fesler
Randy Gradishar
Archie Griffin
Chic Harley
John Hicks
Les Horvath
Jim Houston
Vic Janowicz
Gomer Jones
Jim Parker
Jim Stillwagon
Gaylord Stinchcomb
Jack Tatum
Aurealius Thomas
Bill "Deke" Willis
Gust Zarnas

FOX SPORTS TAILGATING HANDBOOK

Penn State Nittany Lions

RVs arrive early as 6 p.m. Thursday, park in Yellow Lots alongside Orchard and Fox Hollow Roads. Overnight camping $50 per night, first-come, first-served. RV day-only parking $30, cars $15. Tailgating starts 8 a.m. Saturday, continues throughout game. No charcoal or wood grills; gas only. Canopies and tents prohibited in Preferred or Yellow parking areas. No kegs, beer balls or beverage alcohol allowed in parking areas. No oversized inflatables, advertising banners or displays. No weapons or fireworks; no disorderly conduct or infringing on another's area.

School Colors: Blue and White

Stadium: Beaver

Capacity: 107,282

Surface: Grass

Opened: 1960

Phone: (800) 833-5533

Mascot Name: The Nittany Lion

National Championships: (4)–*1911, *1912, 1982, 1986

Heisman Winners: (1)–John Cappelletti (1973)

State College, Pennsylvania

Radio Partners: WMAJ 1450 AM, WMRF 95.7 FM

College Hall of Fame Members:
John Cappelletti
Keith Dorney
Jack Ham
Glenn Killinger
Ted Kwalick
Richie Lucas
Pete Mauthe
Shorty Miller
Lydell Mitchell
Dennis Onkotz
Mike Reid
Glenn Ressler
Dave Robinson
Steve Suhey
Dexter Very
Harry "Lighthorse Harry" Wilson

Shuttle info: Free shuttles are available from downtown and South Atherton St, starting 3 hours before kick-off, until 1 hour post-game.

Purdue Boilermakers

Non-permit RVs can park 6 p.m. Friday night in IM Black Lot, $30. Tailgating starts about 4 hours before game, and continues throughout. No tailgating or shuttle service in free lots. Visit Boilermaker Streetfest alongside Mackey Arena for pre-game family friendly activities, like inflatable games. You can meet the team, too.

School Colors: Old Gold and Black

Stadium: Ross-Ade

Capacity: 62,500

Surface: Grass

Opened: 1924

Phone: (800) 497-7878

Mascot Name: Purdue Pete and Boilermaker Special

National Championships: None

Heisman Winners: None

West Lafayette, Indiana

Radio Partners: WLFF 95.3 FM, WLAS 1410 AM

Shuttle info: Shuttles only available for John Purdue Club members parked in the new U Lot. Shuttle is free.

> **College Hall of Fame Members:**
> Bob Griese
> Cecil "Cece" Isbell
> Leroy Keyes
> Elmer "Ollie" Oliphant

Wisconsin Badgers

RVs and all oversized vehicles park in Lot 51 only, at the corner of Mills and Regent Streets, $40. Purchase parking permits in advance through UW Athletic Ticket Office (608) 262-1440. No overnight parking. Lot 34 is an alcohol-free tailgating zone. Shuttles are provided, $4 roundtrip. Tailgating starts first thing game day, continues throughout game.

School Colors: Cardinal and White

Stadium: Camp Randall

Capacity: 76,634

Surface: Turf

Opened: 1917

Phone: (800) GO-BADGERS

Mascot Name: Bucky Badger

National Championships: (2)–1951, 1958

Heisman Winners: (2)–Alan Ameche (1954), Ron Dayne (1999)

Madison, Wisconsin

Radio Partners: Madison, Wisconsin

College Hall of Fame Members:
Alan "The Horse" Ameche
Kirk Baumgartner
Bob Butler
Pat Harder
Elroy "Crazy Legs" Hirsch
Pat O'Dea
Pat Richter
Dave Schreiner

Shuttle info: Two Bucky Bus shuttle routes run on game day to and from Camp Randall Stadium. Shuttles run every 15 to18 minutes, starting 2 hours prior to kick-off until 1 hour post-game, $4 per person roundtrip. Shuttle picks up at bus stop between Lot 60 and Lot 76, and any of the six Capitol Square parking ramps.

Alabama Birmingham Blazers

Bad news—RVs not allowed in campus lots. Good news—cars $5 per space; extra spaces can be purchased. Arrive early to beat traffic; stay within your space(s).

School Colors: Green, White and Old Gold
Stadium: Legion Field
Capacity: 83,091
Surface: Grass
Opened: 1927
Phone: (205) 975-8224
Mascot Name: Blaze
National Championships: None
Heisman Winners: None
Birmingham, Alabama
Radio Partners: WYDE 101.1 FM, WDJC 850 AM

Shuttle info: No shuttles needed; parking is close to stadium.

Central Florida Knights

Bright House Networks Stadium opens in 2007. While there will be tailgating, the university had not released any rules, pricing, or other details at press time. Call or log on to ucfathletics.cstv.com for details before heading to the stadium.

School Colors: Gold and Black
Stadium: Bright House Networks Stadium
Capacity: 45,000
Surface: Grass
Opened: 2007
Phone: (407) 823-4653
Mascot Name: Knightro
National Championships: None
Heisman Winners: None
Orlando, Florida
Radio Partner: WQTM 740 AM

Shuttle info: The new stadium is on campus. While details had not been announced when this book went to the printer, parking is expected to be within walking distance and no shuttle will be needed.

East Carolina Pirates

Call ahead for RV parking; spaces may be available after 5 p.m. Friday. Call to make arrangements. Parking limited on campus. RVs must be self-contained; no electrical hookups available. No kegs; keep alcohol in cups. Tents allowed for own space only. Stay in your space.

School Colors: Old Gold and Purple

Stadium: Dowdy-Ficklen

Capacity: 43,000

Surface: Grass

Opened: 1963

Phone: (252) 328-4500, (252) 328-4788

Mascot Name: PeeDee the Pirate

National Championships: None

Heisman Winners: None

College Hall of Fame Members: None

Greenville, North Carolina

Radio Partners: WSFL 106.5 FM, WNCT 1070 AM

Shuttle info: Use on-campus Park & Ride lot and take shuttle to stadium, $5. Call -4788 extension to make sure shuttle is running for a specific game.

Houston Cougars

Visitors park in Blue Lot on campus, $5 for cars. RVs stay overnight in Green Lot (space limited). RVs must have special parking pass, $100 to $200. Be prepared for hot weather; bring sunscreen and plenty of water.

School Colors: Scarlet and White
Stadium: Robertson
Capacity: 32,000
Surface: Turf
Opened: 1942
Phone: (713) 743-GOUH
Mascot Name: Shasta
National Championships: None
Heisman Winners: (1)–Andre Ware (1989)
Houston, Texas
Radio Partner: KBME 790 AM

> **College Hall of Fame Members:**
> Andre Ware

Shuttle info: All parking pretty close to stadium. Shuttles aren't needed.

Marshall Thundering Herd

Eleven hundred single-game RV spaces scattered throughout MU parking areas near stadium. RVs pay $10 per space used, first-come, first-served. Just check the signs. No overnight parking. Two blocks west of campus is a parking garage; you can also park on the street. Keep inside your space; no kegs; don't tailgate inside parking garage. (Evidently, someone tried.) Tent City tailgating area half a block from stadium.

School Colors: Green and White
Stadium: Joan C. Edwards
Capacity: 38,019
Surface: Turf
Opened: 1991
Phone: (800) 843-4373
Mascot Name: Marco
National Championships: None
Heisman Winners: None
Huntington, West Virginia
Radio Partners: WDGG 93.7 FM, WVHU 800 AM

College Hall of Fame Members:
Mike Barber
Jackie Hunt
Harry Young

Shuttle info: All parking within easy walking distance. No shuttles needed.

Memphis Tigers

RVs can park a day in advance. May purchase extra parking spaces if needed. No tailgating in handicap spaces. Close to city attractions including Graceland.

School Colors: Blue and Black

Stadium: Liberty Bowl

Capacity: 62,380

Surface: Grass

Opened: 1965

Phone: (901) 729-4344

Mascot Name: Tom the Tiger

National Championships: None

Heisman Winners: None

College Hall of Fame Members: None

Memphis, Tennessee

Radio Partner: WREC 600 AM

Shuttle info: All parking within easy walking distance of stadium; no shuttles needed.

Rice Owls

Tailgaters park in Stadium Lot next to stadium, no charge. No overnight parking; can arrive as early as 9 a.m. on game day. No glass bottles; kegs okay but must be registered with police. For afternoon games you can stay all day; for night games leave by 11 p.m.

School Colors: Navy Blue, Gray, and White

Stadium: Rice

Capacity: 70,000

Surface: Grass

Opened: 1950

Phone: (713) 348-6930

Mascot Name: Sammy the Owl

National Championships: None

Heisman Winners: None

Houston, Texas

Radio Partners: KBME 790 AM, KTRU 91.7 FM

College Hall of Fame Members:
Buddy Dial
Weldon Humble
Dick "Forty-Seven" Maegle
Bill Wallace
James "Froggy" Williams

Shuttle info: Parking is next to stadium, so shuttles aren't needed.

SMU Mustangs

Campus lots reserved for season ticket holders; few spaces left for visitors. Most visitors park downtown and use shuttles. Most tailgating done in grassy picnic area called The Boulevard. Limited space; call ahead. No gas grills allowed.

School Colors: Blue, Red, and White

Stadium: Gerald J. Ford

Capacity: 32,000

Surface: Grass

Opened: 2000

Phone: (214) 768-2582

Mascot Name: Mustang

National Championships: (1)–*1935

Heisman Winners: (1)–Doak Walker (1948)

Dallas, Texas

Radio Partners: KTCK 1310 AM

> **College Hall of Fame Members:**
> Gerald "Little Red Arrow" Mann
> Jerry LeVias
> Don "Dandy Don" Meredith
> Kyle "The Mighty Mustang" Rote
> Doak Walker
> Bobby Wilson

Shuttle info: Free Park & Ride available at Mockingbird Station DART commuter parking lot, located on north side of Mockingbird Lane. Shuttle buses bring you to campus.

Southern Mississippi Golden Eagles

Parking fills up fast; many stake out spots night before. Parking free. No special place for RVs. There's parking on Hillcrest Street, but it's a hike. Keep alcohol concealed.

School Colors: Black and Gold
Stadium: M. M. Roberts
Capacity: 33,000
Surface: Grass
Opened: 1976
Phone: (601) 266-5299 (Eagle Club)
Mascot Name: Seymour D'Campus
National Championships: None
Heisman Winners: None
Hattiesburg, Mississippi
Radio Partners: WFFX 1450 AM

Shuttle info: No special shuttles for game day.

> **College Hall of Fame Members:**
> Ray Guy

Texas-El Paso Miners

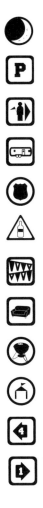

Visiting/single-game RVs park in Schuster Lot A-13 only, $40. RVs can arrive as early as 6 p.m. Friday before game, and stay until 10 a.m. Sunday. Tailgating can continue until end of first quarter; then head for the stadium. After the game, tailgating can resume for one hour. No unofficial power driven vehicles, like golf carts, allowed. No kegs; no live bands, public address systems, or loud stereo systems. No advertising; no selling items or food; no campaigning.

School Colors: Orange, White, and Blue with Silver accent
Stadium: Sun Bowl
Capacity: 51,500
Surface: Turf
Opened: 1963
Phone: (915) 747-5481, (915) 747-5234 (Ticket Center)
Mascot Name: Paydirt Pete
National Championships: None
Heisman Winners: None
College Hall of Fame Members: None
El Paso, Texas
Radio Partner: FOFX 92.3 FM

Shuttle info: Free shuttles available from Lot A-13 to stadium and back. Other shuttle routes around campus drop off at stadium. No drinking in shuttles.

Tulane Green Wave

Tailgating done on top floor of parking garage and on concourse area of Superdome, mostly reserved. Grilling prohibited; no glass containers. Vehicles are not allowed in the Tulane Tailgating Village; you have to park and carry your tailgating gear to your spot. Visit the French Quarter down the street.

School Colors: Green, Blue, Silver, and White
Stadium: Louisiana Superdome
Capacity: 69,767
Surface: Turf
Opened: 1975
Phone: (504) 861-WAVE, (504) 587-3633 (Superdome)
Mascot Name: Riptide
National Championships: None
Heisman Winners: None
New Orleans, Louisiana
Radio Partner: WIST 690 AM

Shuttle info: You're in downtown New Orleans. Use city's public transit system.

College Hall of Fame Members:
Bill Banker
Jerry Dalrymple
John Green
Lester Lautenschlaeger
Eddie Price
Monk Simons

Tulsa Golden Hurricanes

Visitor parking on north end of campus off 5th Street; short walk to stadium. RVs park night before; no hookups, but free. Stay in front of or behind your vehicle. Tents must be 10 x 10 feet or smaller. No grilling during fire alerts. Porta-potties, trash service provided.

School Colors: Old Gold, Royal Blue, and Crimson
Stadium: Skelly
Capacity: 40,385
Surface: Turf
Opened: 1930
Phone: (918) 631-2935
Mascot Name: Captain Cain
National Championships: None
Heisman Winners: None
Tulsa, Oklahoma
Radio Partner: KRMG 740 AM

College Hall of Fame Members:
Glenn Dobbs
Jerry Rhome
Howard Twilley

Shuttle info: No shuttle service offered during football games.

Army Black Knights

Tailgating starts 8 a.m. game day. RVs park in Red, Blue, or Green Lots; MPs will direct you to appropriate lot. Single-game parking free, but it's a hike to the stadium. Use the shuttle. No weapons or hazardous items. Security very strict; you must have photo ID on person at all times. All vehicles will be searched. Hey, at least you're safe.

School Colors: Black, Gray, and Gold

Stadium: Michie

Capacity: 40,000

Surface: Turf

Opened: 1924

Phone: (845) 446-0538

Mascot Name: Black Knight

National Championships: (3)–1914, 1944, 1945

Heisman Winners: (3)–Doc Blanchard (1945), Glenn Davis (1946), Pete Dawkins (1958)

West Point, New York

Radio Partner: WEPN 1050 AM

Shuttle info: Free shuttles are available; use color code of lot (red, blue, green) for correct bus.

College Hall of Fame Members:
Bob Anderson
Doc "Mr. Inside" Blanchard
Paul Bunker
Chris "Red" Cagle
Bill "The Lonely End" Carpenter
Charlie Daly
Glenn "Mr. Outside" Davis
Pete Dawkins
Arnold Galiffa
Edgar Garbisch
John Green
Don Holleder
Harvey Jablonsky
Doug Kenna
John McEwan
Frank Merritt
Robin Olds
Elmer Oliphant
Barney Poole
Bud Sprague
Joe Steffy
Alex Weyand

Navy Midshipmen

Single-game RV parking is limited, and presold before game day. Call ticket office for a spot, $45 if available. RVs use Gate 1 at north end of stadium to get to parking areas. Tailgating allowed on Navy-Marine Corps Memorial property only. Cars can park $15 at Germantown Elementary School lot. Park & Ride lots scattered throughout downtown. No overnight parking, saving spaces, or fireworks. Keep your grill as small as possible.

School Colors: Blue and Gold
Stadium: Memorial
Capacity: 30,000
Surface: Grass
Opened: 1959
Phone: (800) 874-6289 (Ticket Office)
Mascot Name: Bill the Goat
National Championships: None
Heisman Winners: (2)–Joe Bellino (1960), Roger Staubach (1963)
Annapolis, Maryland
Radio Partner: WNAV 1430 AM

Shuttle info: Free shuttle service with your ticket on *any* City of Annapolis bus.

College Hall of Fame Members:
Ron Beagle
Joe Bellino
Buzz Borries
George Brown
John "Babe" Brown
Slade Cutter
John Dalton
Dick Duden
Steve "Ike" Eisenhauer
Tom Hamilton
Jonas Ingram
Napoleon McCallum
Skip Minisi
Bob Reifsnyder
Clyde Scott
Dick Scott
Roger "Roger the Dodger" Staubach
Don Whitmire
Frank Wickhorst

Notre Dame Fighting Irish

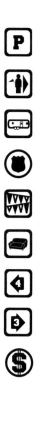

RVs park in White Field, $60. No overnight parking available. Cars park for $20. No tailgating during game; propane grills limited to 20 tank and smaller; no charcoal grills; no kegs allowed. Vehicles remaining in lots longer than 3 hours towed.

School Colors: Blue, Gold, and White

Stadium: Notre Dame

Capacity: 80,795

Surface: Grass

Opened: 1930

Phone: (574) 631-7356

Mascot Name: The Leprechaun

National Championships: (11)–1924, 1929, *1930, 1943, 1946, 1947, 1949, *1966, *1973, 1977, 1988

Heisman Winners: (6)–Angelo Bertelli (1943), John Lujack (1947), Leon Hart (1949), John Lattner (1953), John Huarte (1964), Tim Brown (1987)

South Bend, Indiana

Radio Partner: WNDV 92.9 FM

Shuttle info: TRANSPO Shuttle Buses begin limited service (2 buses) to Library Circle, north of ND Stadium, when White Field opens. Service will increase to 12 buses as game time approaches; these run into first half, with a minimum of 1 bus running during game. Postgame, 14 buses run in sets of 4 from Library Circle back to White Field. Shuttles run until lines cease or at least 1 hour after game's end (whichever is longer). Two buses will run up to 3 hours longer, based on need.

College Hall of Fame Members:
Hunk Anderson
Angelo "Springfield Rifle" Bertelli
Ross Browner
Jack Cannon
Frank Carideo
George Connor
Jim Crowley
Zygmont Czarobski
Bob "Grandpappy" Dove
Ray Eichenlaub
Bill "Moose" Fischer
George "The Gipper" Gipp
Jerry Groom
Ralph "Goog" Guglielmi
Leon Hart
Frank Hoffmann
Paul "The Golden Boy" Hornung
John Huarte
Johnny Lattner
Elmer "The Thin Man" Layden
Johnny Lujack
Jim Lynch
Ken MacAfee
Jim Martin
Bert Metzger
Creighton Miller
Don "Midnight" Miller
Edgar "Rip" Miller
Fred Miller
Wayne Millner
Alan Page
Louis "Red" Salmon
Marchy Schwartz
William Shakespeare
Red "Six-Yard" Sitko
John "Clipper" Smith
Harry Stuhldreher
Joe Theismann
Adam Walsh
Bob Williams
Tommy Yarr

Temple Owls

University and stadium in downtown Philadelphia so parking decentralized. Some parking within walking distance. Make sure you have a Philly cheesesteak while you're here.

School Colors: Cherry and White

Stadium: Lincoln Financial Field

Capacity: 68,532

Surface: Grass

Opened: 2003

Phone: (215) 204-6267

Mascot Names: Hooter and T-Bird

National Championships: None

Heisman Winners: None

College Hall of Fame: None

Philadelphia, Pennsylvania

Radio Partner: WPHT 1210 AM

Shuttle info: You're in the middle of Philadelphia. Use Philly's public transit system.

Akron Zips

Stadium is off campus. RVs park next to Lot 3, only $5. Tailgating done in grassy areas; no overnight parking, but prices are affordable. No kegs where people can see them; no glass; propane grills only. University prefers fans not tailgate during games. No glass rule strictly enforced.

School Colors: Blue, Gold, and White
Stadium: Rubber Bowl
Capacity: 35,202
Surface: Turf
Opened: 1940
Phone: (888) 99-AKRON
Mascot Name: Zippy the Kangaroo
National Championships: None
Heisman Winners: None
College Hall of Fame: None
Akron, Ohio
Radio Partner: WARF 1350 AM

Shuttle info: Shuttle service free, starts 3 hours prior to game and runs until 1 hour after game's end.

Ball State Cardinals

RVs, buses, and oversized vehicles (not pickups) park in baseball parking lot, $5 a vehicle. No overnight parking. Tailgating begins 3 hours prior to kickoff. No kegs or hard liquor allowed; legal drinkers use discretion. Couches and other indoor furniture are prohibited. Lawn furniture is just fine. No tents larger than 10 x 10 feet allowed. Grill your heart out, but dispose of charcoal properly: cooked grass is never a pretty sight. Leave the banners at home.

School Colors: Cardinal and Cream
Stadium: Ball State
Capacity: 21,581
Surface: Grass
Opened: 1967
Phone: (765) 285-1474
Mascot Name: Charlie Cardinal
National Championships: None
Heisman Winners: None
College Hall of Fame: None
Muncie, Indiana
Radio Partners: WKJG 1380 AM

Shuttle info: All parking close to stadium. Shuttles not necessary.

Bowling Green Falcons

Separate lots for donors and visitors. Tailgate Park, adjacent to stadium, sells hospitality tents for $200–$1,000 to groups. Visitors park on campus for $5, RVs for $10. RVs can arrive up to two days early.

School Colors: Brown and Orange
Stadium: Doyt Perry
Capacity: 30,599
Surface: Grass
Opened: 1966
Phone: (806) 742-4260
Mascot Names: Freddie and Frieda
National Championships: None
Heisman Winners: None
College Hall of Fame: None
Bowling Green, Ohio
Radio Partner: WBUK 106.3 FM

Shuttle info: All parking within walking distance. No shuttles needed.

Buffalo Bulls

No overnight parking. Keep alcohol in cups; leave keg at home.

School Colors: Liberty Blue and White

Stadium: UB

Capacity: 31,000

Surface: Grass

Opened: 1993

Phone: (716) 645-3177

Mascot Names: Victor E. Bull and Victoria S. Bull

National Championships: None

Heisman Winners: None

College Hall of Fame: None

Buffalo, New York

Radio Partner: WGR 550 AM

Shuttle info: All parking within walking distance of stadium; no shuttle needed.

Central Michigan Chippewas

RV owners call ahead for overnight permit or game-day parking. Tailgate next to your vehicle. Families can purchase tailgating packages from the university—get table, chairs, etc.; set up in grassy area near pond. No pull-behind grills, kegs, or glass bottles. Tents used in designated areas only. Tailgating ends when game begins.

School Colors: Maroon and Gold
Stadium: Kelly-Shorts
Capacity: 30,199
Surface: Turf
Opened: 1972
Phone: (888) Fire-Up-2 (347-3872)
Mascot Name: None
National Championships: None
Heisman Winners: None
College Hall of Fame: None
Mount Pleasant, Michigan
Radio Partner: WMHW 91.5 FM

Shuttle info: Parking's close by stadium. No shuttles needed.

Eastern Michigan Eagles

RVs can arrive 5 hours before game, and begin tailgating at Porter Park. Leave glass containers and kegs at home. Alcohol may be brought in 10 ounce cans, or 12 ounce plastic bottles. Each person can carry a maximum of 6 cans/bottles. Got a case? Split it up between 4 friends to carry. Any more than 6 cans/bottles per person will be considered a gift for security personnel.

School Colors: Green and White
Stadium: Rynearson
Capacity: 30,200
Surface: Turf
Opened: 1969
Phone: (734) 487-2282
Mascot Name: Swoop
National Championships: None
Heisman Winners: None
College Hall of Fame: None
Ypsilanti, Michigan
Radio Partner: WEMU 89.1 FM

Shuttle info: All parking close to stadium. Shuttles not needed.

Kent State Golden Flashes

General parking available in lots south of stadium. Additional parking available along East Summit Street, in campus parking lots, and in former Giant Eagle parking lot on State Route 59, across from Gabriel Brothers. Be discreet with alcohol. Tailgate Alley features live entertainment, food and beverages, inflatables, interactive games, and appearances by Flash and Kent State cheerleaders—all for free.

School Colors: Blue and Gold
Stadium: Dix
Capacity: 30,520
Surface: Turf
Opened: 1969
Phone: (330) 672-3350
Mascot Name: Flash
National Championships: None
Heisman Winners: None
College Hall of Fame: None
Kent, Ohio
Radio Partner: WHK 1420 AM

Shuttle info: All parking areas serviced by free shuttles to and from Dix Stadium.

Miami (Ohio) Redhawks

Up to 4 hours before game parking is free; afterward cars pay $7, RVs $14. RVs park in RV City. No overnight parking; no alcohol allowed.

School Colors: Red and White

Stadium: Fred Yager

Capacity: 30,112

Surface: Grass

Opened: 1983

Phone: (513) 529-1620

Mascot Name: Swoop

National Championships: None

Heisman Winners: None

College Hall of Fame: None

Oxford, Ohio

Radio Partner: WMOH 1450 AM

Shuttle info: No shuttles needed. Parking is close to stadium.

Northern Illinois Huskies

Parking lots open 3 hours prior to kickoff. All buses, motor homes, and RVs are required to park in Lot C3 of the Convocation Center, $15. No overnight parking. No tailgating during the game. No glass; use cans and plastic bottle beverages only. You must obtain a permit to use a tent.

School Colors: Cardinal and Black
Stadium: Huskie
Capacity: 31,000
Surface: Turf
Opened: 1965
Phone: (815) 753-1923
Mascot Name: Victor E. Huskie
National Championships: None
Heisman Winners: None
DeKalb, Illinois
Radio Partner: WLBK 1360 AM

Shuttle info: Trolleys and carts get tailgaters from Convocation Center to stadium.

> **College Hall of Fame Members:**
> George Bork

Ohio Bobcats

Most tailgating done in Pepsi Tailgate Park grass lot. Alcohol allowed only there and requires a permit; can't buy extra spaces. RVs must park in cement lots, but can buy extra spaces. No overnight parking. No tents. Leave at the end of the game.

School Colors: Hunter Green and White
Stadium: Pedan
Capacity: 24,000
Surface: Grass
Opened: 1929
Phone: (740) 597-1358, (740) 593-4491, (740) 597-1375
Mascot Name: Rufus the Bobcat
National Championships: None
Heisman Winners: None
College Hall of Fame: None
Athens, Ohio
Radio Partner: WXTQ 105.5 FM

Shuttle info: No shuttles needed. Parking is close to stadium.

Toledo Rockets

Tailgating done in two specified lots; call for locations. No alcohol, but not firmly enforced rule. No glass bottles or overnight parking.

School Colors: Midnight Blue and Gold

Stadium: Glass Bowl

Capacity: 26,248

Surface: Turf

Opened: 1937

Phone: (419) 530-3611

Mascot Name: Rocky the Rocket

National Championships: None

Heisman Winners: None

Toledo, Ohio

Radio Partner: WSPD 1370 AM

College Hall of Fame Members:
Merle Gulick
Mel Long

Shuttle info: No shuttles needed. Parking is close to stadium.

Western Michigan Broncos

Parking at Waldo Stadium is extremely limited; fans should park at Lawson Ice Arena and ride free shuttle service to the Stadium. Game-day parking $5 per vehicle. No overnight parking. No glass containers, kegs, or couches (lawn furniture fine). One space per vehicle. Tailgating stops when game begins.

School Colors: Brown and Gold
Stadium: Waldo
Capacity: 30,200
Surface: Grass
Opened: 1950
Phone: (269) 387-8092
Mascot Name: Buster Bronco
National Championships: None
Heisman Winners: None
College Hall of Fame: None
Kalamazoo, Michigan
Radio Partners: WFAT 96.5 FM, WZUU 92.3 FM

Shuttle info: Free shuttle service runs continuously from Lawson Ice Arena to Waldo Stadium starting 3 hours before kickoff. Shuttle runs continuously throughout game from Gate 4 area at east end of stadium on Oakland Drive.

Air Force Falcons

New lots include Lot 2A, Lot 2, Lot 3, and Lot 4; you'll be directed to the appropriate lot. Parking's free, but you must call ahead to reserve spot. Large parties call events management—space very limited. No tailgating items restricted.

School Colors: Blue and White
Stadium: Falcon
Capacity: 52,480
Surface: Grass
Opened: 1962
Phone: (719) 472-1895, (719) 333-9021 (Events Management)
Mascot Name: The Bird
National Championships: None
Heisman Winners: None
Colorado Springs, Colorado
Radio Partner: KVOR 740 AM

....
: **College Hall of Fame Members:** :
: Brock Strom :
....

Shuttle info: Parking is close to stadium. No shuttles needed.

Brigham Young Cougars

Single-game RVs park in Lot 37, northwest of Smith Fieldhouse, $25. RVs can park overnight for weekend games, not on weekdays. Most fans leave 2 hours after game; RVs can spend the night. No alcohol, tobacco, or open fires. Dispose of coals safely. BYU fans use Dutch ovens on grills or coals for great dishes. Local fans are very friendly—enjoy it.

School Colors: Blue and White

Stadium: LaVell Edwards

Capacity: 65,000

Surface: Grass

Opened: 1964

Phone: (801) 422-2028

Mascot Name: Cosmo the Cougar

National Championships: (1)–1984

Heisman Winners: (1)–Ty Detmer (1990)

Provo, Utah

Radio Partner: KSL 1160 AM

College Hall of Fame Members:
Jim McMahon
Gifford Nielsen
Marc Wilson
Steve Young

Shuttle info: Parking is close to stadium. No need for shuttles.

Colorado State Rams

All parking outside stadium in huge unpaved lot. Vistiting RVs have section just for them, but not overnight. A few lots reserved for large parties (50 people). Visiting team fans have their own tailgate area—call ahead to arrange. Use plastic cups for drinks; use canopies, not spiked tents.

School Colors: Forest Green, Gold, and White
Stadium: Hughes
Capacity: 30,000
Surface: Grass
Opened: 1963
Phone: (970) 491-6020
Mascot Name: Cam the Ram
National Championships: None
Heisman Winners: None
Fort Collins, Colorado
Radio Partner: KCOL 600 AM

College Hall of Fame Members:
Thurman McGraw

Shuttle info: Parking is adjacent to stadium. Shuttles not needed.

New Mexico Lobos

RV parking available in any open lot except Tailgate 2 Lot. All parking free; donors get parking priority. Visitors park in lots around campus. No overnight parking; no glass containers, party balls, or kegs; no commercial tailgating. You must have a ticket to the game to tailgate. No tailgating during game. Must pack up and leave 30 minutes after game's end.

School Colors: Cherry and Silver
Stadium: University
Capacity: 37,730
Surface: Grass
Opened: 1960
Phone: (505) 925-LOBO
Mascot Name: Lobo Louie and Lucy
National Championships: None
Heisman Winners: None
College Hall of Fame: None
Albuquerque, New Mexico
Radio Partner: KKOB 770 AM

Shuttle info: Parking is close to stadium. Shuttles aren't needed.

San Diego State Aztecs

Qualcomm Stadium off campus, located on Friars Road. Parking surrounds stadium. Parking free before 1 p.m.; after that it's $7. No alcohol allowed. Tailgating family oriented; visit Fun Zone for children's activities, live music, and more.

School Colors: Scarlet and Black
Stadium: Qualcomm
Capacity: 70,561
Surface: Grass
Opened: 1967
Phone: (619) 283-7378
Mascot Name: Aztec Warrior
National Championships: None
Heisman Winners: None
San Diego, California
Radio Partners: XEPE 1700 AM, XEPE 105.7 FM, XEPRS 1090 AM

> **College Hall of Fame Members:**
> George Brown
> Fred Dryer

Shuttle info: Parking surrounds stadium. Shuttles not needed.

TCU Horned Frogs

RVs park night before game on campus RV lot; $50 for weekend.
Parking, tailgating spots vary in distance, but there are shuttles.
No open fires; alcohol must be concealed.

School Colors: Purple and White

Stadium: Amon Carter

Capacity: 44,008

Surface: Grass

Opened: 1929

Phone: (817) 257-5658

Mascot Name: Super Frog

National Championships: (1)–1938

Heisman Winners: (1)–Davey O'Brien (1938)

Ft. Worth, Texas

Radio Partner: KESN 103.3 FM

College Hall of Fame Members:
Ki Aldrich
Sammy "Slingin' Sammy" Baugh
Darrell Lester
Bob Lilly
Rags Matthews
Davey "Slingshot" O'Brien
Jim Swink

Shuttle info: Free parking and shuttle service available to stadium
from Paschal High School and Sandage Lot. Service begins 2
hours prior to game time and runs continuously for 45 minutes
after end of game.

University of Nevada–Las Vegas Running Rebels

RVs park for free, but not on the grass and not overnight. Actually, all general parking is free. Kegs are okay; no glass containers; no grills or open pit fires. Game times may change due to weather or ESPN schedule.

School Colors: Scarlet and Grey
Stadium: Sam Boyd
Capacity: 36,800
Surface: Grass
Opened: 1971
Phone: (702) 895-15337
Mascot Name: Hey Reb
National Championships: None
Heisman Winners: None
College Hall of Fame: None
Las Vegas, Nevada
Radio Partner: KSHP 1400 AM

Shuttle info: Student shuttles bring students from campus to games and back. General parking close enough; shuttles aren't necessary.

Utah Utes

Visitors park in various lots; season ticket holders use official tailgate lot. Get your tailgate pass with your ticket. Overnight parking available except for Thursday games. No alcohol.

School Colors: Crimson and White
Stadium: Rice-Eccles
Capacity: 45,634
Surface: Grass
Opened: 1927
Phone: (801) 581-8849
Mascot Name: Swop
National Championships: None
Heisman Winners: None
College Hall of Fame: None
Salt Lake City, Utah
Radio Partner: KALL 700 AM

Shuttle info: Take Utah Transit Authority TRAX directly to stadium. Use Rally & Ride lots at 10000 South, 5200 South, and the 4th South Market (400 South 600 East), near University Line Trolley Station. Fans can park in those lots as early as 2 p.m.

Wyoming Cowboys

General parking is $10 per game in Lot X, off 19th Street, and baseball lot off 30th and Willett. Tailgating okay in all lots, but only donor lots can have alcohol (open containers). Alcohol available (for legal drinkers only) in Pepsi's Cowboy Tailgate Park. Pepsi's Tailgate Park has festival atmosphere with huge vendor tents, food for sale, etc. All tailgating stops 30 minutes before kickoff.

School Colors: Brown and Gold
Stadium: War Memorial
Capacity: 33,500
Surface: Grass
Opened: 1950
Phone: (307) 766-4850
Mascot Name: Cowboy Joe and Pistol Pete
National Championships: None
Heisman Winners: None
Laramie, Wyoming
Radio Partner: KEVA 1240 AM

College Hall of Fame Members:
Eddie "Boom Boom" Talboom

Shuttle info: All parking close to stadium. No shuttles needed.

Arizona Wildcats

Tailgating begins 5 hours before kickoff, and must be cleared away 1 hour after game's end. RV parking (tailgating pass) is $70, cars $55. Tailgate on grassy areas at UA Mall, Gittings Lawn, or McKale Lawn. Due to construction, most of McKale Lawn unavailable for 2007. Only beer and wine allowed. No generators, glass containers, kegs, or hard liquor. Free parking available for carpool vehicles (4 or more people) at Highland Avenue and Sixth Street Garages, and all vehicles at Park Avenue Garage.

School Colors: Cardinal and Navy
Stadium: Arizona
Capacity: 56,500
Surface: Grass
Opened: 1928
Phone: (520) 621-3710
Mascot Name: Wilbur the Wildcat
National Championships: None
Heisman Winners: None
Tucson, Arizona
Radio Partner: KCUB 1290 AM

College Hall of Fame Members:
Ricky Hunley

Shuttle info: All parking within easy walking distance. Shuttles aren't needed.

Arizona State Sun Devils

RVs park in Lot 4. Some lots are free, others charge up to $40. Parking opens 7 a.m. game day; tailgating starts 3 1/2 hours before kickoff and stops during game. Lots must be cleared 1 hour after game's end. No glass containers or hard liquor; only beer and wine allowed. All parking is within walking distance to stadium.

School Colors: Maroon and Gold
Stadium: Sun Devil
Capacity: 73,379
Surface: Grass
Opened: 1928
Phone: (480) 965-2381
Mascot Name: Sparky
National Championships: None
Heisman Winners: None
Tempe, Arizona
Radio Partners: KTAR 620 AM, KMVP 860 AM, KDUS 1060 AM

College Hall of Fame Members:
Michael "Luxury" Haynes
John Jefferson
Danny White

Shuttle info: All parking within easy walking distance. Shuttles aren't needed.

California Golden Bears

Parking around stadium for season ticket holders. Public parking sold on first-come, first-served basis. City and private lots offer parking near campus and in downtown. Cost varies from free to $50. New tailgate area for 2007 at Claremont Middle School at 5750 College Avenue. Cost is $15 per spot. No grilling inside parking garages; obey city ordinances on drinking, noise, etc.

School Colors: Blue and Gold
Stadium: Memorial
Capacity: 73,347
Surface: Turf
Opened: 1923
Phone: (800) 462-3277, (888) CAL-ALUM
Mascot Name: Oski
National Championships: (3)–1920, *1921, *1922
Heisman Winners: None
Berkeley, California
Radio Partner: KGO 810 AM

Shuttle info: Free shuttles run from Park & Ride lots, starting 2 hours before game and continuing 1 hour after game's end.

College Hall of Fame Members:
Sam "Tiburon Terror" Chapman
Rod Franz
Walter Gordon
Matt Hazeltine
Bob Herwig
Edwin "Babe" Horrell
Jackie Jensen
Joe Kapp
Dan McMillan
Craig Morton
Harold "Brick" Muller
Les Richter
Ed "The Goose" White

Oregon Ducks

All stadium RV parking reserved for donors. Donors can arrive Friday night, park overnight. For single game RVs, use Park & Ride lots. For a really big tailgate party, check out the Ed Moshofsky Sports Center—it's got everything you could imagine.

School Colors: Green and Yellow
Stadium: Autzen
Capacity: 54,000
Surface: Turf
Opened: 1967
Phone: (541) 346-4461
Mascot Name: Donald Duck
National Championships: None
Heisman Winners: None
Eugene, Oregon
Radio Partner: KUGN 590 AM

Shuttle info: Shuttles pick up passengers at Park & Ride lots; shuttle is $3.

> **College Hall of Fame Members:**
> Terry Baker
> John "Jack" Beckett
> Johnny "Flying Dutchman" Kitzmiller
> Mel Renfro
> Norm "The Dutchman" Van Brocklin

Oregon State Beavers

RVs can arrive 5 p.m. Friday, and stay until Sunday afternoon. Most parking is reserved for donors, but some pay parking is available on first-come, first-served basis. No kegs allowed. Tailgating during game allowed. Benton County Fairground's free RV parking best bet for visiting RVs (there is a fee for hookups). Visit free Fan Fair at Beaver Boulevard, starting 3 hours before kickoff.

School Colors: Orange and Black
Stadium: Reser
Capacity: 35,362
Surface: Turf
Opened: 1953
Phone: (800) GO BEAVS
Mascot Name: Benny Beaver
National Championships: None
Heisman Winners: (1)–Terry Baker 1962
Corvalis, Oregon
Radio Partner: KEX 1190 AM

> **College Hall of Fame Members:**
> Terry Baker

Shuttle info: A free fairground shuttle runs 3 hours prior to and 1 hour after game.

Stanford Cardinal

Donor RVs park in El Camino Grove, as early as Friday evening before game. Visiting RVs are out of luck; best bet is to park in Stanford Shopping Center, walk to stadium. Most parking lots are free, but some charge a fee. Dispose of coals properly.

School Colors: Cardinal and White

Stadium: Stanford

Capacity: 85,500

Surface: Grass

Opened: 1921

Phone: (800) STANFORD

Mascot Name: The Stanford Tree (Unofficial)

National Championships: (1)–*1926

Heisman Winners: (1)–Jim Plunkett (1970)

Stanford, California

Radio Partner: KZSU 90.1 FM

Shuttle info: All parking within easy walking distance. No shuttles necessary.

College Hall of Fame Members:
Frankie Albert
John Brodie
Chris Burford
Bill "The Baby Faced Assassin" Corbus
John Elway
Hugh "Duke" Gallarneau
Bobby Grayson
Bob "Bones" Hamilton
Bill McColl
James Moscrip
Ernie "Big Dog" Nevers
Jim Plunkett
Bob "Horse" Reynolds
Chuck Taylor
Paul Wiggin

UCLA Bruins

No overnight parking, but you can tailgate during the game. Overnighters and other RVs should go to Parpark lot at 100 W. Walnut Street. $50 per night; parking on first-come, first-served basis starting at 7 a.m. Tents larger than 10 x 10 feet need city permit; keep propane tanks away from brush. Parking is within walking distance, but there are shuttles available.

School Colors: Gold and Blue
Stadium: Rose Bowl
Capacity: 91,500
Surface: Grass
Opened: 1922
Phone: (310) UCLA WIN
Mascot Name: Joe Bruin and Josephine Bruin
National Championships: (1)– *1954
Heisman Winners: (1)–Gary Beban (1967)
Los Angeles, California
Radio Partner: KLAC 570 AM

Shuttle info: Rose Bowl provides free shuttle service to and from game, from all Parpark lots.

> **College Hall of Fame Members:**
> Gary "The Great One" Beban
> Kenny Easley
> Tom Fears
> Billy Kilmer
> Donn Moomaw
> Jerry Robinson
> Al Sparlis
> Kenny "Kingfish" Washington

USC Trojans

RVs park in Lot 2 across from Coliseum, $125 per day. Overnight parking is sometimes available, call Classic Parking for info. Starting 3 hours before game, shuttles are provided from campus and downtown. Tailgating during game allowed. No tent stakes or commercial signage; no amplified sound; no open flame under tents, trees, or inside parking garages. Security checks entering stadium are lengthy. Come early.

School Colors: Cardinal and Gold
Stadium: Los Angeles Memorial Coliseum
Capacity: 92,000
Surface: Grass
Opened: 1923
Phone: (213) 747-7111, (213) 749-5654 (Classic Parking)
Mascot Names: Traveler, Tommy Trojan
National Championships: (10)–*1928, 1931, *1932, 1962, 1967, 1972, *1974, *1978, *2003, 2004
Heisman Winners: (7)–Mike Garrett (1965), O. J. Simpson (1968), Charles White (1979), Marcus Allen (1981), Carson Palmer (2002), Matt Leinart (2004), Reggie Bush (2005)
Los Angeles, California
Radio Partner: KSPN 710 AM

Shuttle info: A free shuttle runs from USC Parking Center (Jefferson and Grand) to Coliseum (39th and Figueroa) starting 3 hours before game time.

College Hall of Fame Members:
Marcus Allen
Jon "Jaguar Jon" Arnett
John Baker
Ricky Bell
Tay Brown
Brad Budde
Paul Cleary
Anthony Davis
Morley Drury
John Ferraro
Mike "Iron Mike" Garrett
Frank Gifford
Mort Kaer
Ronnie Lott
Mike McKeever
Dan McMillan
Erny Pinckert
Marvin Powell
Aaron Rosenberg
Ernie Smith
Harry Smith
Lynn Swann
Cotton Warburton
Charles White
Ron Yary
Charles "Tree" Young

Washington Huskies

RVs park in Lot E1, for $40, but not overnight. Parking is "stacked" (bumper to bumper) so you don't leave until the guy in front of you does. When tailgating, use as little space as possible. No reserving spaces. No alcohol (adults use discretion). At U of W fans "sterngate": up to 5,000 people in Lake Washington tailgating on boats. Very cool.

School Colors: Purple and Gold

Stadium: Husky

Capacity: 72,500

Surface: Turf

Opened: 1920

Phone: (206) 543-2210

Mascot Name: Harry the Husky

National Championships: (1)–*1991

Heisman Winners: None

Seattle, Washington

Radio Partner: KJR 950 AM

College Hall of Fame Members:
Chuck Carroll
Don Heinrich
Vic Markov
Hugh "The King" McElhenny
Rick Redman
Bob Schloredt
Paul Schwegler
Max Starcevich
George "Wildcat" Wilson

Shuttle info: All parking within easy walking (swimming?) distance. No shuttles needed.

Washington State Cougars

RVs park in designated lots, behind Indoor Practice Facility and across from South Fairway Playfield, as early as 5 p.m., Thursday. No tents, tables, or chairs are permitted in parking spaces or on sidewalks. Tables and chairs under an RV awning are okay. Be aware of town's open container law. Don't dump charcoal in Dumpsters or trash cans. Throw trash away properly.

School Colors: Crimson and Gray
Stadium: Clarence D. Martin
Capacity: 37,600
Surface: Turf
Opened: 1972
Phone: (800) Go COUGS
Mascot Name: Butch T. Cougar
National Championships: None
Heisman Winners: None
Pullman, Washington
Radio Partner: KXLY 920 AM

College Hall of Fame Members:
Glen Edwards
Mel Hein

Shuttle info: Several shuttle options for Cougar fans—Pullman Transit provides free bus service on home football game days. Along with normal transit service and campus shuttles two Express routes and a new Visitor Center/Downtown shuttle is offered. Starting 3 hours prior to kickoff and running continuously until 1 1/2 hours after the game. Call Pullman Transit at (509) 332-6535 or the WSU Visitor Center at (509) 335-8633 for more information.

Alabama Crimson Tide

Tailgaters can arrive as early as 6 p.m. Friday, depart no later than noon on Sunday. Stadium parking reserved for donors, season ticket holders. Tailgaters gather on the Quad, adjacent to Gorgas Library. RVs tailgate in Lots 1 through 9. No stakes/spikes may be used to secure tents or canopies—use sandbags if needed. Buses park for free on 12th Street. Shuttles run from off-campus to stadium, provided by Tuscaloosa Transit Authority.

School Colors: Crimson and White

Stadium: Bryant-Denny

Capacity: 83,818

Surface: Grass

Opened: 1929

Phone: (205) 348-6113 (Tide Pride), (205) 348-8391 (Parking Services)

Mascot Name: Elephant

National Championships: (10)– *1925, *1926, *1930, *1961, 1964, *1965, *1973, *1978, 1979, 1992

Heisman Winners: None

Tuscaloosa, Alabama

Radio Partners: WZRR 99.5 FM, WJOX 690 AM, WZBQ 94.1 FM, WRTR 105.5 FM

College Hall of Fame Members:
Cornelius Bennett
Johnny Mack Brown
John Cain
Harry Gilmer
John Hannah
Dixie Howell
Pooley Hubert
Don Hutson
Lee Roy Jordan
Vaughn "Cisco" Mancha
Johnny "The Italian Stallion" Musso
Billy Neighbors
Ozzie "The Wizard of Oz" Newsome
Fred Sington
Riley "General" Smith
Don Whitmire

Shuttle info: Shuttles run from University Mall (10th Avenue across from Stadium), $10, and from downtown across from AmSouth Bank, $4.

Arkansas Razorbacks

RVs arrive as early as Wednesday before game, park at Road Hog Park at Razorback Road and 15th, $20-30 per day. Cars park for free in any non-reserved lot and in grassy areas adjacent to lots, also at the Gardens. Keep tailgating within your parking space. Don't use tent spikes. Tailgating allowed from 7 a.m.–9 p.m.

School Colors: Cardinal and White
Stadium: Razorback
Capacity: 80,000
Surface: Grass
Opened: 1938
Phone: (479) 575-4412
Mascot Names: Tusk, Sue E. Pig, Boss Hogg
National Championships: (1)–*1964
Heisman Winners: None
Fayetteville, Arkansas
Radio Partners: KABZ 103.7 FM, KARN 102.9 FM & 920 AM

> **College Hall of Fame Members:**
> Lance "Bambi" Alworth
> Chuck Dicus
> Wayne "The Thumper" Harris
> Loyd Phillips
> Wear Schoonover
> Clyde "Smackover" Scott
> Billy Ray Smith

Shuttle info: Free shuttles available from public parking at Baum Stadium and Baldwin Piano to a Bud Walton Arena drop-off before the game (buses will return to those areas after the game). Shuttles start 4 hours before kickoff, running until all fans are returned to their vehicles.

Auburn Tigers

RVs can arrive as early as 4 p.m. Wednesday, first-come, first-served, park in grass lots on corner of Donahue Drive and Lem Morrison Drive. Parking is free. Tailgating allowed all day game day in any non-reserved lot and in core of campus. No amplified sound-systems; no tent stakes longer than 12 inches. No grilling on parking decks. Grills must be 50 feet away from ANY campus structure.

School Colors: Burnt Orange and Navy Blue

Stadium: Jordan Hare

Capacity: 86,063

Surface: Grass

Opened: 1939

Phone: (800) AUB-1957

Mascot Name: Aubie

National Championships: (1)–*1957

Heisman Winners: (2)–Pat Sullivan (1971), Bo Jackson (1985)

Auburn, Alabama

Radio Partners: WKKR 97.7 FM

> **College Hall of Fame Members:**
> Terry Beasley
> Tucker Frederickson
> Walter Gilbert
> Jimmy Hitchcock
> Bo Jackson
> Tracy Rocker
> Pat Sullivan

Shuttle info: All parking within easy walking distance. No shuttles needed.

Florida Gators

RVs can arrive 6 p.m. Friday, and park for free at Park & Ride lot next to Hilton Hotel, off 34th Street. RV parking first-come, first-served. Tailgating starts 6 a.m. game day; doesn't stop until noon Sunday when everybody leaves. Open container laws STRICTLY enforced.

School Colors: Orange and Royal Blue
Stadium: Florida Field
Capacity: 90,000
Surface: Grass
Opened: 1929
Phone: (352) 375-4683
Mascot Name: Albert E. Gator and Alberta
National Championships: (2)–1996, 2006
Heisman Winners: (2)–Steve Spurrier (1966), Danny Wuerffel (1996)
Gainesville, Florida
Radio Partners: WAFC 106.3 FM, WVOI 1480 AM

College Hall of Fame Members:
Steve Spurrier
Dale Van Sickel
Jack Youngblood

Shuttle info: RTS Gator Aider provides shuttle service from multiple off-campus locations, $6 per game, $30 per season. Shuttles run 3 hours before kickoff, until 1 hour after game ends.

Georgia Bulldogs

RVs arrive 6 p.m. Friday; park at Prestige Parking three blocks away from stadium. RV parking is $75 a weekend. Tailgating starts as early as 7 a.m. game day and ends 2 hours after game. Alcohol is limited to North Campus Quad and D. W. Brooks Mall. Tailgaters must provide own power source. Alcohol-free, family-friendly areas available in North and South campus.

School Colors: Red and Black
Stadium: Sanford
Capacity: 92,746
Surface: Grass
Opened: 1929
Phone: (706) 542-7275, (706) 357-9613 (Prestige Parking)
Mascot Name: UGA (IV) , Spike
National Championships: (2)–*1942, 1980
Heisman Winners: (2)–Frank Sinkwich (1942), Herschel Walker (1982)
Athens, Georgia
Radio Partners: WSB 750 AM

Shuttle info: All parking within easy walking distance. No shuttles needed.

College Hall of Fame Members:
Kevin Butler
Bill Hartman
Terry Hoage
Bob McWhorter
John Rauch
Frank "Fireball Frankie" Sinkwich
Vernon "Catfish" Smith
Bill Stanfill
Fran Tarkenton

Kentucky Wildcats

RVs start arriving Friday at 6 p.m., park for free on Press Avenue. Early RV arrivals wait in holding area at the Soccer/Softball lot. Parking attendant will issue early RVs a number upon arrival. RVs then released into Press Avenue lot in numerical order when area opens. Any campus parking lot designated "E" available after 3:30 p.m. on Friday (unless otherwise posted) and all day Saturday and Sunday. Non-reserved disabled lot located at the corner of University Drive and Farm Road—free shuttles provided. Tailgating starts 8 a.m. game day, ends at day's end. Golf carts allowed in RV lots only. No open alcoholic containers at stadium. The following items require prior approval: oversized grills, banners/signage recognizing businesses, generators, tents over 10 x 10 square feet.

School Colors: Blue and White

Stadium: Commonwealth

Capacity: 67,530

Surface: Grass

Opened: 1973

Phone: (800) 928-CATS

Mascot Names: Blue, The Wildcat, Scratch

National Championships: None

Heisman Winners: None

Lexington, Kentucky

Radio Partners: WLAP 630 AM, WBUL 98.1 FM

College Hall of Fame Members:
Bob Gain
Lou Michaels
Babe Parilli

Shuttle info: Free shuttle service available from Press Avenue and Tobacco Research Building to Stadium.

LSU Tigers

Visiting RVs park in Vet Med lot, open 7 a.m. Friday. Parking $100 per game, not per day. Overflow RV parking at Farr Park, 2 miles south of campus. Call (225) 769-7805 to make arrangements. Tailgating starts as early as 7 a.m. game day, until 2 hours after game. All tailgating areas within walking distance of the stadium. No tents larger than 10 x 10 feet allowed; all music must be turned off by midnight pregame, and by 2 a.m. postgame. No portable generators; no cookers larger than a 55-gallon drum.

School Colors: Purple and Gold
Stadium: Tiger
Capacity: 92,300
Surface: Grass
Opened: 1924
Phone: (225) 578-2184
Mascot Name: Mike (V)
National Championships: (2)–*1958, 2003
Heisman Winners: (1)–Billy Cannon (1959)
Baton Rouge, Louisiana
Radio Partner: WDGL 98.1 FM

College Hall of Fame Members:
Tommy Casanova
Doc Fenton Mansfield
Ken Kavanaugh
Abe "Miracle" Mickal
Gaynell "Gus" Tinsley

Shuttle info: All parking within easy walking distance. No shuttles needed.

Mississippi Rebels

Traveling RVs arrive 5 p.m. Friday, park free in three non-reserved areas—intramural fields off Hawthorne Road (gated entrance behind Gillom Sports Center), gravel lot at corner of Old Taylor Road and Highway 6, and Food Management Institute parking lot off Hill Drive. Tailgating at The Grove starts 12 a.m. Saturday, ends 12 a.m. Sunday. No tent stakes. No generators, no open flames of any kind, no propane grills, no alcohol (keep in cup, be discreet).

School Colors: Cardinal Red and Navy Blue
Stadium: Vaught-Hemingway
Capacity: 60,580
Surface: Grass
Opened: 191
Phone: (662) 915-7167
Mascot Name: None (Colonel Reb—Unofficial)
National Championships: (1)—*1960
Heisman Winners: None
Oxford, Mississippi
Radio Partner: WCJU 1450 AM

College Hall of Fame Members:
Charlie "Chuck'n Charlie" Conerly
Charlie "Flavy" Flowers
Jake Gibbs
Parker "Bullet" Hall
Bruiser Kinard
Archie Manning

Shuttle info: All parking within easy walking distance. No shuttles needed.

Mississippi State Bulldogs

RVs park as early as noon Friday in non-reserved lots on Stone Boulevard, past Spring Street/Blackjack Road. RVs vacate by 7 a.m. Sunday, or 7 a.m. next day of classes. RVs pay $40 for weekend passes, available on-site. Cars pay $5 or $10 in lots near Bully Boulevard, Dudy Noble Field, and adjacent to unreserved RV lots. Other lots are free. Tailgating starts as early as 5 p.m. Friday for weekend or holiday games, or 5 hours before weekday games. Don't park on grass or obstruct traffic or parking areas. Tents limited to 12 x 12 feet. No tents, tables, or chairs in parking spaces or on sidewalks. Charcoal grills allowed. Follow state and local laws on alcohol. Picnic areas in Picnic Zone are first-come, first-served.

School Colors: Maroon and White
Stadium: Davis Wade
Capacity: 55,082
Surface: Grass
Opened: 1915
Phone: (662) 325-8121
Mascot Name: Bully
National Championships: None
Heisman Winners: None
Starkville, Mississippi
Radio Partner: WFCA 107.9 FM

> **College Hall of Fame Members:**
> D. D. Lewis
> Jackie Parker

Shuttle info: Free shuttle service available from Thad Cochran Research and Economic Development Park (north of Hwy 182) from campus. Shuttles will run 2 hours prior to game time and continue until 2 hours after game's end.

South Carolina Gamecocks

RVs and cars park at State Fairgrounds, adjacent to stadium. (Stadium's not on campus.) Parking is close to stadium. RVs may arrive 5 p.m. Friday. Weekend parking $75, or $40 for game day only. Cars pay $15 to $20 (based on proximity to stadium). Tailgating starts 7 a.m. game day, runs until midnight after game. No campfires or open flames (grills are okay). USC now has Gamecock Village, with former players signing autographs, live entertainment, games, food and beverages, USC cheerleaders, and mascot. Gamecock Village located in grandstands at State Fair Grounds, open 3 hours prior to kickoff.

School Colors: Garnet and Black

Stadium: Williams Brice

Capacity: 80,250

Surface: Grass

Opened: 1934

Phone: (803) 799-3387 (South Carolina State Fairgrounds)

Mascot Name: Cocky

National Championships: None

Heisman Winners: (1)–George Rogers (1980)

Columbia, South Carolina

Radio Partners: WTCB 106.7 FM, WISW 1320 AM

Shuttle info: All parking within easy walking distance. No shuttles needed.

> **College Hall of Fame Members:**
> George Rogers

Tennessee Volunteers

There's no general parking on campus. Visiting RVs can park at the Civic Coliseum and at Blackstock Street lot behind Foundry at North World's Fair area. Cost is $25 per day, accommodating about 100 RVs, with hookups for 20. Shuttle service is provided. Tailgating starts 7 a.m. game day, runs until midnight after game. When tailgating off-campus, all local and state laws apply, and are enforced. No alcohol, open fires, or tents. Visit Volunteer Village, open 3 1/2 hours before game, with interactive games, live bands, autographs, cheerleaders, and WNOX's Sports-talk "Game Day All Day."

School Colors: Orange and White

Stadium: Neyland

Capacity: 104,079

Surface: Grass

Opened: 1921

Phone: (865) 974-6031

Mascot Name: Smokey (IX)

National Championships: (2)–1951, 1958

Heisman Winners: None

Knoxville, Tennessee

Radio Partners: WNOX 990 AM, WIVK 107.7 FM

College Hall of Fame Members:
Doug Atkins
George Cafego
Steve DeLong
Bobby Dodd
Nathan Dougherty
Frank Emanuel
Beattie Feathers
Herman Hickman
Bob Johnson
Steve Kiner
Hank Lauricella
Johnny Majors
Gene McEver
John Michels
Ed Molinski
Joe Steffy
Bob Suffridge
Reggie "Minister of Defense" White
Bowden Wyatt

Shuttle info: Shuttles start 3 hours prior to game time. Shuttles run from Blackstone Lot at World Fair Park, also from Coliseum, Old City, and Market Square area of downtown, $4 per person, round trip. Shuttles also running from Farragut High School, $10 per person round trip.

Visiting RVs park as early as 5 p.m. Friday at Harris-Hillman School on Blakemore in Lots 106, 107, 108. RVs may stay overnight for $50, or 2 nights for $62. Cars may park on game day for $5. Cars can park at Dudley Stadium for free, or in Lots A and T for $10. Tailgating starts 7 a.m. game day, runs until midnight after game. No parking in grass or restricted areas. In Harris-Hillman lots, no amplified music or alcohol allowed. In Vandy lots no glass bottles.

School Colors: Black and Gold
Stadium: Vanderbilt
Capacity: 39,790
Surface: Grass
Opened: 1981
Phone: (615) 322-GOLD
Mascot Name: Mr. C
National Championships: None
Heisman Winners: None
Nashville, Tennessee
Radio Partners: WSM 650 AM & 95.5 FM

College Hall of Fame Members:
Lynn Bomar
Josh Cody
Carl Hinkle
Bill Spears
John Tigert

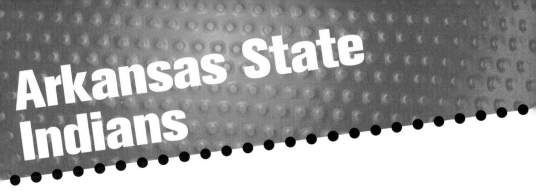

Arkansas State Indians

RVs park in lots south of stadium starting Friday night; can stay until Sunday. Ten RV spots have hookups, $15 day. No alcohol; must leave by midnight. Lots of golf courses nearby—bring your clubs.

School Colors: Scarlet and Black
Stadium: Indian
Capacity: 33,410
Surface: Grass
Opened: 1974
Phone: (870) 972-3930
Mascot Name: Red
National Championships: None
Heisman Winners: None
College Hall of Fame: None
Jonesboro, Arkansas
Radio Partners: KEWI 690 AM

Shuttle info: Parking is close to stadium. Shuttles not needed.

Florida Atlantic Owls

General parking is $5 in lots surrounding stadium (off campus); parking is first-come, first-served. Tailgating spaces are limited to 10 x 8-foot spaces provided. No overnight parking allowed. No kegs; no glass containers. No generators, DJs, or home speakers; no golf carts or motorized scooters. No catering. After game, tailgating can continue for 1 hour, but parking is allowed for 3 hours. Remember, you're on private property—be polite.

School Colors: Blue, Red and Silver
Stadium: Lockhart
Capacity: 20,450
Surface: Grass
Opened: 1959
Phone: (866) FAU-OWLS
Mascot Name: Burrowing Owl
National Championships: None
Heisman Winners: None
College Hall of Fame: None
Boca Raton, Florida
Radio Partners: WJNA 640 AM

Shuttle info: No shuttles needed. Parking is close to stadium.

Florida International Golden Panthers

Hey, parking's free. RVs park and set your tailgate up in Lot 6, at west end of lot. Lot 7 reserved for donors. Tailgating can continue through game, but must end 1 hour after game's end.

School Colors: Blue and Gold
Stadium: FIU
Capacity: 17,000
Surface: Turf
Opened: 1995
Phone: (866) FIU-GAME
Mascot Name: Roary the Panther
National Championships: None
Heisman Winners: None
College Hall of Fame: None
Miami, Florida
Radio Partner: WKAT 1360 AM

Shuttle info: Parking pretty close to stadium. No shuttles needed.

Louisiana-Lafayette Ragin' Cajuns

Cajun Field is off campus, but parking is nearby. Reserved RV and tailgating areas are for season ticket holders. Visitors park in a large first-come, first-served parking area. No glass containers, open fires, 4-wheelers, or motorcycles.

School Colors: Vermilion and White
Stadium: Cajun Field
Capacity: 31,000
Surface: Grass
Opened: 1971
Phone: (337) 482-5393
Mascot Name: Cayenne
National Championships: None
Heisman Winners: None
College Hall of Fame: None
Lafayette, Louisiana
Radio Partner: KRVS 88.7 FM

Shuttle info: Parking is close to stadium. Shuttles aren't needed.

Louisiana–Monroe Warhawks

Most parking restricted; some lots for visitors to tailgate. RVs may arrive Thursday evening. Keep inside your space.

School Colors: Maroon and Gold

Stadium: Malone

Capacity: 30,427

Surface: Grass

Opened: 1978

Phone: (318) 342-3ULM

Mascot Name: Chief Brave Spirit

National Championships: None

Heisman Winners: None

College Hall of Fame: None

Monroe, Louisiana

Radio Partners: KJLO 104.1 FM, KMLB 1440 AM

Shuttle info: Shuttles aren't needed. Parking is close to stadium.

RVs can park the night before. There are parking lots, grass lots, and parking on local streets, all nearby. No alcohol on campus. Leave by Sunday night. Visit Hillbilly Hilton for some serious tailgaters.

School Colors: Royal Blue and White
Stadium: Floyd
Capacity: 30,788
Surface: Turf
Opened: 1933
Phone: (615) 898-2210
Mascot Name: Lightning
National Championships: None
Heisman Winners: None
College Hall of Fame: None
Murfreesboro, Tennessee
Radio Partners: WNFN 106.7 FM, WGNS 1450 AM

Shuttle info: Raider Express shuttles fans from outer parking lots to stadium. When getting on bus, tell driver you're going to game. You'll be dropped off at stadium. Buses run every 15 minutes.

North Texas Eagles

Single-game RVs arrive Friday night, park in Orange Lot, $50. There's also some first-come, first-served parking on North Texas Boulevard. Don't use tent stakes. Mean Green Village has music, food, fun, and good kid-stuff. No glass containers, kegs, or pets anywhere, and no vehicles in Mean Green Village. Please clean up your trash, okay?

School Colors: Green and White

Stadium: Fouts Field

Capacity: 30,500

Surface: Turf

Opened: 1952

Phone: (940) 565-2527, (940) 369-7643

Mascot Name: Scrappy

National Championships: None

Heisman Winners: None

Denton, Texas

Radio Partner: KTCK 1310 AM

College Hall of Fame Members:
Joe "Mean Joe" Greene

Shuttle info: Texas may be big, but UNT's parking and stadium areas aren't. No shuttles needed.

Troy Trojans

All campus parking reserved for donors, season ticket holders. One RV lot on campus without hookups for visitors and single-game ticket holders. Parking available in town; cost varies. RVs should leave by Sunday afternoon. No kegs or glass containers; keep drinks in cups.

School Colors: Cardinal, Black, and Silver
Stadium: Movie Gallery Veterans
Capacity: 30,000
Surface: Turf
Opened: 1950
Phone: (877) 878-9467
Mascot Name: T-Roy
National Championships: None
Heisman Winners: None
College Hall of Fame: None
Troy, Alabama
Radio Partners: WTBF 94.7 FM & 970 AM

Shuttle info: Everything's within walking distance. No need for shuttles.

Boise State Broncos

Parking on campus really limited. Visitors can park downtown in parking garages, $5; Washington Group International Parking Structure, $5; on residential streets; or on campus on first-come, first-served basis. RVs call -3560 extension for parking pass. Vehicles can't park longer than 48 hours on residential streets. Obey town ordinances. No open containers of alcohol. Tailgating concludes 30 minutes before kickoff.

School Colors: Blue and Orange
Stadium: Bronco
Capacity: 30,000
Surface: Turf
Opened: 1970
Phone: (208) 426-4737, (208) 426 3560
Mascot Name: Buster Bronco
National Championships: None
Heisman Winners: None
Boise, Idaho
Radio Partner: KBOI 670 AM

> **College Hall of Fame Members:**
> Randy Trautman

Shuttle info: Boise's town shuttle free with game ticket. Shuttle stops include corner of 6th and Grove, corner of 8th and Idaho, and corner of 10th and Main, plus others.

Fresno State Bulldogs

Single-game RVs park in Gray Lot, $150. Call ahead for spot. Alcohol permitted in only three college-owned tailgating areas, Gray, Red, and White Lots; other areas are state property. Tents must be 10 x 10 feet or smaller. No charcoal grills, no kegs. No tailgating during game. Some of this may change—call after the first week of June to check.

School Colors: Cardinal and Blue
Stadium: Bulldog
Capacity: 41,031
Surface: Grass
Opened: 1980
Phone: (559) 278-DOGS
Mascot Name: Timeout
National Championships: None
Heisman Winners: None
College Hall of Fame: None
Fresno, California
Radio Partner: KMJ 580 AM

Shuttle info: Shuttle runs from east side, charges a "nominal" fee.

Hawaii Rainbows

Tailgating in specific lots available on first-come, first-served basis. Don't tailgate in other stadium lots. No reserving or saving parking spaces. No dumping coals/ashes, pegging tents, or throwing balls or Frisbees in parking area.

School Colors: Green, Black and Silver

Stadium: Aloha

Capacity: 50,000

Surface: Turf

Opened: 1975

Phone: (808) 486-9500

Mascot Name: Vili the Warrior

National Championships: None

Heisman Winners: None

College Hall of Fame: None

Honolulu, Hawaii

Radio Partners: KKEA 1420 AM

Shuttle info: Use TheBus, a popular public transit system serving the entire Island of Oahu.

Idaho Vandals

Parking is generally located on the west end of the Dome in Blue Lot #57 and Red Lot #34. RVs can park ahead of time; call -6424 extension to make arrangements. You must have game ticket to park in West lots and tailgate. No alcohol allowed, but game ticket gets you into alumni area, where beer and food are sold. Visit official tailgating events with food, music, and kid stuff. Leave immediately after game.

School Colors: Black and Gold
Stadium: Kibbie Dome
Capacity: 16,000
Surface: Turf
Opened: 1975
Phone: (208) 885-6466, (208) 885-6424, (208) 885-0200
Mascot Name: Joe Vandal
National Championships: None
Heisman Winners: None
College Hall of Fame: None
Moscow, Idaho
Radio Partners: KTIK 1350 AM

Shuttle info: Free shuttles are available for larger games, not smaller ones.

Louisiana Tech Bulldogs

Park your car or RV; bring everything to specified tailgating areas (wheeled coolers are a good idea here). RVs have specific lots for parking; can arrive 48 hours before game. No alcohol. Visit Tailgate Alley with music and food in a carnival atmosphere.

School Colors: Red and Reflex Blue
Stadium: Joe Aillet
Capacity: 30,600
Surface: Grass
Opened: 1968
Phone: (318) 257-4111
Mascot Names: Tech XIX and Champ
National Championships: None
Heisman Winners: None
Ruston, Louisiana
Radio Partner: KXKZ 107.5 FM

College Hall of Fame Members:
Terry Bradshaw

Shuttle info: Parking close by stadium. Shuttles not needed.

Nevada Wolf Pack

Parking is still free, woo-hoo! RVs park in Lot R1 Friday after 6 p.m., stay until 6 p.m. Sunday. No kegs or party-balls; tents can be rented. No tailgating in covered garages. Dispose of hot coals safely (not on grass, dirt, or pavement, or in trashcans). Hey, you can kayak downtown!

School Colors: Cobalt Blue and Silver
Stadium: Mackay
Capacity: 31,900
Surface: Grass
Opened: 1967
Phone: (775) 784-6900 ext. 293
Mascot Name: Alphie
National Championships: None
Heisman Winners: None
Reno, Nevada
Radio Partner: KPTT 630 AM

....
College Hall of Fame Members:
Frank Hawkins
....

Shuttle info: Several shuttles available from downtown Park & Ride lots, and from Scruples, Bully's, and the BrewHouse. All free.

New Mexico State Aggies

All tailgating done in a single large, unpaved lot east of stadium. Visiting RVs can arrive a day early. No kegs allowed; no glass, keep alcohol in cups. Have your ID handy; they check 'em at random. Come tailgate 5 hours prior to kickoff at Aggie Air Raid Tailgate park.

School Colors: Crimson and White
Stadium: Aggie Memorial
Capacity: 30,343
Surface: Grass
Opened: 1978
Phone: (505) 646-2569
Mascot Name: Pete
National Championships: None
Heisman Winners: None
College Hall of Fame: None
Las Cruces, New Mexico
Radio Partner: KVLC 101.1 FM

Shuttle info: All parking pretty close to stadium. Shuttles aren't needed.

San Jose State Spartans

RV parking available in Fan Fiesta Lot on 10th and Alma Street fence line on first-come, first-served basis. You're charged by number of spaces you take up, $15 per space. RVs need 2 spaces. No alcohol after kickoff time. All tents stored in secure area before entering stadium. Normally, overnight parking not allowed. But overnight parking might be arranged—call ahead to see if overnight parking in Lot 6A, north end of Bud Winter Field, is possible.

School Colors: Blue and Gold
Stadium: Spartan
Capacity: 30,456
Surface: Grass
Opened: 1933
Phone: (408) 924-7589
Mascot Name: Sammy the Spartan
National Championships: None
Heisman Winners: None
San Jose, California
Radio Partners: KNTS 1220 AM

College Hall of Fame Members:
Willie Heston

Shuttle info: Parking on street opposite stadium. You totally don't need a shuttle.

Utah State Aggies

No overnight parking; no alcohol or glass containers.

School Colors: Aggie Blue

Stadium: Romney

Capacity: 30,257

Surface: Grass

Opened: 1968

Phone: (435) 797-1860

Mascot Name: Big Blue

National Championships: None

Heisman Winners: None

Logan, Utah

Radio Partners: KVNU 610 AM

College Hall of Fame Members:
Merlin Olsen

Shuttle info: Parking close by stadium. Shuttles not needed.

RESOURCES

General Information

Before you head to the stadium, you may need more information on throwing a great tailgate party, or where to find the stuff with which to do it. For tailgating tips (including game-day and travel checklists), podcasts, videos, and recipes visit my Web site, theultimatetailgater.com. You can also find all sorts of helpful tools and information about tailgating from the American Tailgaters Association at atatailgate.com. The ATA is a national organization that promotes tailgating, offers members discounts on tailgating supplies and gear, reviews tailgating products, provides information for tailgating at stadiums coast-to-coast, and more.

PRODUCTS MENTIONED IN THE BOOK

TOP 5 GRILLS:

Weber Q: weber.com/bbq

Freedom Grill FG-50: freedomgrill.com

Thermos Grill 2 Go: grill2go.com

Woodflame Delecto: woodflame.com/en/delecto.php

Solaire Anywhere Infrared Grill: rasmussen.biz/grills/portG.html

TOP 5 SMOKERS:

Weber Smokey Mountain Cooker Smoker: weber.com/bbq

Brinkmann Smoke 'N Pit Pitmaster: brinkmann.net

Brinkmann Smoke 'N Grill Gas: brinkmann.net

Bar-B-Chef Charcoal Smoker: bbqgalore.com

Bradley Smoker (Original): bradleysmoker.com

TOP 5 COOLERS:

Rubbermaid 5-Day Endurance Cooler: rubbermaid.com

Rubbermaid 13.2 Qt. Slim Cooler: rubbermaid.com

Igloo Cool Fusion 40 Ice Tunes: igloocoolers.com

California Innovations All Terrain Rolling Cooler: ca-innovations.com

WAECO CoolFreeze: waecousa.com

TOP 5 TAILGATE CHAIRS:

Take-a-Seat: thetakeaseat.com

Hammaka Sports Chair: hammaka.com/interface.htm

Insta-bench: insta-bench.com

Tailgate Chair with Side Table: americantailgater.com (search "chair side table")

Texsport Folding Picnic Table with Umbrella: texsport.com

TOP 5 TAILGATE TOYS:

Cruzin Cooler: cruzincooler.com

Tailgator Gas Powered Blender: totallygross.com

The Daiquiri Whacker: gasblender.com

The Beer Belly: thebeerbelly.com

Sippin' Seat: papabert.com

OTHER PRODUCTS:

Griddle Q: littlegriddle.com

Clean BBQ Grill Covers: cleanbbq.com

Honda Generator (EU1000i): hondapowerequipment.com/genpum.htm

Sports Fan Tailgate Table: booneoutdoorhardware.com/tailgatetable.html

E-Z Up Instant Shelter: ezup.com

Other Tailgating Supplies

GRILLS & ACCESSORIES

Before buying it's a good idea to compare features and options to make sure you get the best grill for your style of tailgating. Some good sources of information and research are:

bbq.about.com/od/grills/index.htm?terms=grills

consumersearch.com/www/sports_and_leisure/gas-grill-reviews/index.html

npba.org

With all that knowledge, you're ready to get your grill. Here are some sites for tailgating grills and accessories:

bbqgalore.com

brinkmann.net

campchef.com

campingworld.com

ducane.com

freedomgrill.com

grillingaccessories.com

grilllovers.com

homedepot.com

lowes.com

webergrills.com

TENTS

All across the America you'll find a sea of tents outside stadiums. For many tailgaters a canopy is enough. But for others, tents with sides and other options make for the ultimate tailgate party. You can find a variety of tents on these Web sites:

canopycenter.com

elitedeals.com/nctatelocate.html

eurekatents.com

ezupdirect.com

kdkanopy.com

shopping.com/xGS-Tailgating_Tents

GENERAL TAILGATING SUPPLIES

From licensed products to coolers to tables to chairs to . . . you get the idea.

americantailgater.com

collegegear.com

footballfanatics.com

tailgatehq.com

tailgatepartyshop.com

tailgatetown.com

tailgatingsupplies.com

PARTY DECORATIONS

To turn your parking spot into a parking lot party you need to dress it up. In addition to food, drinks, and friends, party lights, banners, and pom-poms help.

4funparties.com

bulkpartysupplies.com

party411.com

partyoptions.net/party_supply/football-main-page.htm

partypro.com

partyshelf.com/football.htm

Stephen Linn is the author of The Ultimate Tailgater series of books and host of a number of podcasts and shows for and about tailgaters. His other books include:

The Ultimate Tailgater's SEC Handbook

The Ultimate Tailgater's ACC Handbook

The Ultimate Tailgater's Big 12 Handbook

The Ultimate Tailgater's Big Ten Handbook

The Ultimate Tailgater's Pac-10 Handbook

The Ultimate Tailgater's Handbook

The Ultimate Tailgater's Travel Guide

The Ultimate Tailgater's Racing Guide

On his Web site, **theultimatetailgater.com**, you'll find Stephen's blog, tailgating videos, podcasts, recipes, contests, and more!